A TASTE OF
SWITZERLAND

A TASTE OF
SWITZERLAND

SUE STYLE

Photographs by John Miller

HEARST BOOKS
NEW YORK

For the Badger,
who makes the best fondue in the business

Text copyright © 1992 by Sue Style
Photographs copyright © 1992 by John Miller, except for those
photographs credited on page 158
Map by David Williams copyright © 1992 by Pavilion Books

The moral right of the Author has been asserted

Published in the United States of America in 1992 by William
Morrow and Company, Inc., 1350 Avenue of the Americas,
New York, N.Y., 10019

First published in Great Britain in 1992 by Pavilion Books
Limited, 196 Shaftesbury Avenue, London, WC2H 8JL, England

Book design by Janet James

Library of Congress Cataloging-in-Publication Data

Style. Sue.
A taste of Switzerland / Sue Style.
p. cm.
Includes index.
ISBN 0-688-10900-4
1. Cookery, Swiss. 2. Switzerland – Social life and customs.
3. Switzerland – Description and travel – 1981–   . I. Title.
TX723.5.S9S88 1992
641.59494–dc20   92-9665
CIP

Printed and bound in Germany by Mohndruck

First U.S. Edition
1 2 3 4 5 6 7 8 9 10

The Publishers gratefully acknowledge the support of 'Cheeses
from Switzerland' in the making of this book

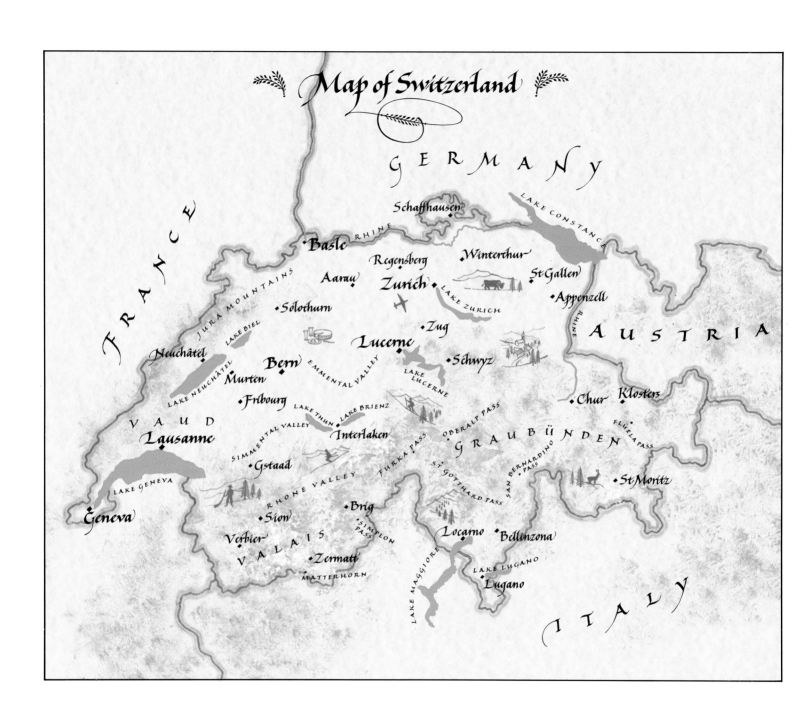

C O N T E N T S

INTRODUCTION

Switzerland needs no introduction. Most people know that this tiny country of some six million inhabitants sits, landlocked, in the middle of Europe overlooked by neighbours as disparate as Italy, France, Germany and Austria. Many are familiar with Swiss bank notes (built to last), Swiss cheese (impressively holey), and Swiss chocolate (the best, they say, in the world). Some are even aware that about three-quarters of the Swiss population speaks German, less than a quarter have French as their mother tongue, that a few speak Italian, and a proud handful Romansch.

But what of the taste of Switzerland, its food, its wines, its gastronomic traditions and history? How can one even talk of the taste of a country which is, in fact, at least four countries rolled into one, not to mention the outside influences from its northern, eastern, southern and western neighbours? There is, of course, no such thing as Swiss food, rather a series of cantonal specialities and gastronomic traditions built up over centuries around a number of home-grown staples such as milk, cheese, cereals, pork, vegetables (particularly potatoes), fruit and wine. Though the food may vary in character from Lucerne to Lausanne, from Chur to Chiasso, it will be carefully prepared, efficiently served and almost invariably delicious. One of the

Left: Early evening sunlight in the
Chur valley.
Above: A fine example of sgraffiti decoration
peculiar to the Engadine region

dangerously comforting facts of Helvetian life is that it is quite difficult to find a bad meal.

My own tastes of Switzerland, during ten years spent here, have been deliciously diverse. The après-skiing reward of a slab of rich chocolate cake or a fragile fruit pastry, and unfailingly delicious coffee with a thick layer of creamy foam on top; a rich ointment of golden onions oozing out of a pastry case for a 4 a.m. breakfast on a February morning at the start of Basle's famous carnival; steaming risotto and sausages on the piazza down in Ticino on Martedi Grasso; a summer raclette amongst the wild flowers outside the alpine hut of wine-growing friends in the Valais, prepared against an open fire and served with home-grown tomatoes, new potatoes in their skins and wine from the valley; Swiss National Day barbecues of sausages criss-crossed at both ends and impaled on freshly whittled sticks; magnificent meringues for an autumn birthday treat in the Emmental, sandwiched with ice cream, further embellished with whipped cream and liberally splashed with apple Schnapps; risotto with thumbnail-sized chanterelles for a well-earned walkers' lunch in the Engadine; home-baked Christmas cookies – chocolate, shortbread, anis- and cinnamon-flavoured – offered in beribboned boxes. And always, at any table, serious slices of freshly-cut bread, white, wholewheat, rye or a mixture. Tastings of Swiss wine from Thurgau to Ticino complete the gastronomic picture, conducted in cellars, on garden walls, even (memorably) inside a supine wine vat. Staple foods, simple pleasures, robust flavours . . . These are the real tastes of Switzerland.

THE BIRTH OF SWITZERLAND

The territory now known as Switzerland was originally settled in the north and west by Celts (who called their land Helvetia) and in the east by Etruscans (who called theirs Raetia). Half a century before the birth of Christ, the Romans marched up over the Alps and colonized the entire area from the Rhone valley to Basle, from the Engadine to lake Constance. Their influence, which was to extend over four centuries, was a civilizing one: they tapped hot springs to make baths (many of them still in use today), built senate houses, theatres, palaces and arches, grew asparagus, introduced apples, plums, pears and cherries, sowed cabbages, courgettes (zucchini) and peas, and cultivated herbs and spices. They tamed the wild vines and made wine. With the decline of the Roman Empire, the ethnic and linguistic foundations of present-day Switzerland were laid: the 'barbarians' (Alemanns) took over northern and eastern Switzerland (today's German-speaking areas) while the Burgundians settled in the west of the country (now the French-speaking cantons). The Alemanns did not succeed in penetrating as far as the mountain regions of eastern Switzerland, so the little enclave of Raetia (part of which is now Graubunden) remained intact; here various Raeto-Romanic dialects are still spoken. Beyond the alps to the south was the Italian-speaking area.

Under the Holy Roman Empire, Switzerland had several different rulers: the northern part was answerable to southern Germany

A spectacular
view of the
Engadin.

(Swabia), the western part to Burgundy, present-day Ticino to the lords of Como and Milan, while Raetia was (as ever) fiercely independent. Few towns of note existed in the Middle Ages, but there were numerous abbeys such as that of St Gallen, famous for its cultured community and its library of illuminated manuscripts. Many of the religious communities grew their own food and wine and regularly provided board and lodging to weary travellers. They were the early forerunners of the Swiss hoteliers.

After the collapse of the Holy Roman Empire, Switzerland was left in the hands of a number of ruling families (notably the Lenzburgs, Kyburgs, Zähringens and Hapsburgs), each of which dominated a different region. Of these, by far the most important were the Hapsburgs, with whom the Swiss were to fight intermittently and fiercely over the next four hundred years. (Some might say the battle still rages between the Swiss and the Austrians, though nowadays it is usually of a verbal nature.) An historic showdown came when the imperial family, who through shrewd intermarrying and inheritance had already gained rights over large chunks of central Switzerland and bought up the town of Lucerne, then proceeded to introduce tolls on traffic over the all-important Gotthard pass. In 1291, the hard-pressed inhabitants of the three original forest states (Uri, Schwyz and Unterwalden) – themselves responsible for building the pass – could stand it no longer. United in defiance of the Hapsburgs, they assembled on the Rütli meadow by lake Lucerne to swear an eternal pact of mutual help and protection. The pact concluded with the vow that the regulations contained therein would 'for the common good and welfare, by God's will, endure forever'. It served as the cornerstone on which the Swiss Confederation was built, and whose seven hundredth anniversary was celebrated in 1991.

Bern, capital city of the Confederation.

THE CONFEDERATION EXPANDS

The Hapsburgs were not (yet) to be outdone, however, and the empire struck back first at Morgarten in 1315, later at Sempach in 1386 and again at Naefels in 1388. Each time they were defeated by the increasingly emboldened Swiss, whose reputation as fearsome fighters was fast becoming legendary. Finally the Swiss demanded and received a charter from the emperor, to be subsequently and successively renewed, recognizing their right to live in peace. Lucerne, their market town at the top of the lake, was soon to join them and the

three states became four. Gradually the association was enlarged to include Zurich followed by Zug, Glarus and Bern in 1353. Later, in 1481, came Fribourg and Solothurn, followed in 1501 by Basle and Schaffhausen. In 1513 the adherence of tiny Appenzell brought the numbers of Confederates to thirteen in all.

While central Switzerland was busy keeping the Hapsburgs at bay, elsewhere the House of Savoy held sway from lake Geneva up to Fribourg, and around the Rhône into the Valais as far upstream as Saillon. On the western flank there were some notable battles with Charles the Bold, Duke of Burgundy at Murten and Grandson in which the Swiss were victorious; in Italy, however, they were roundly defeated at Marignano in 1515. In 1521 the Swiss decided to opt for armed neutrality, a status which has persisted to this day. The Reformation, preached in Zurich by Zwingli and in Geneva by Calvin threatened to tear apart the fragile alliance of the thirteen confederates, some of whom wished to embrace reform, others of whom wanted to remain Catholic. An important compromise was reached whereby the principle of religious freedom was established. By the time the Thirty Years War broke out a century later, the Swiss, fearing that this conflict on their borders would break their own Confederation, remained neutral. (Demand for Swiss mercenaries abroad, however, continued unabated; a last remnant of this tradition is still to be found in the Swiss Guard at the Vatican which is staffed by Swiss soldiers.) At the end of the war, Swiss independence and sovereignty was recognized by Louis XIV and the defeated German emperor.

FROM HELVETIAN REPUBLIC TO SWISS CONSTITUTION

The French showed scant respect for Switzerland's newly won independence and sovereignty and after the Revolution Napoleon invaded, proclaimed the Helvetian Republic and imposed centralized rule, a device wholly unsuited to – and firmly resisted by – the

democratic (and decentralized) Swiss. The country became a battleground between France and its enemies. With the Act of Mediation in 1803, the Helvetian Republic was abolished and replaced with a confederation of the thirteen former member states, plus six new ones: Aargau, St Gallen, Graubunden, Thurgau, Ticino and Vaud. After Napoleon's ignominious defeats in Russia and at Leipzig (this despite large numbers of Swiss mercenaries), the French withdrew. The Valais (pre-

Early morning purchases at Basle market.

13

viously a French *département*) was liberated, Neuchâtel was returned to its previous owner the King of Prussia, and Geneva also became – briefly – independent. These three were to join the Confederation in 1815, making twenty-two cantons in all. Each had its own system of weights and measures, legal system, currency and postal service – Europe, in fact, in miniature.

At the conclusion of the last major skirmish on Swiss soil (a religious conflict known as the Sonderbund war), a new constitution was drawn up in 1848, one currency was adopted for the whole country, a unified system of weights and measures and a national postal service introduced and customs barriers abolished between cantons. At the end of the nineteenth century a period of considerable prosperity began. Switzerland was 'discovered' by the British and other travellers, railways, roads and tunnels were built, alpine tourism was born. Finally in 1975 the twenty-third canton of Jura was formed.

Flags of the Confederation in the streets of Chur, Graubunden.

THE TASTES OF SWITZERLAND

How different are the tastes of the twenty-three cantons? They can be loosely divided along their linguistic lines: the Swiss Germans, the French-speakers, the Italian speakers – and Graubunden. A whole book could be (and many have been) written about the latter canton alone which rubs mountainous shoulders with both Austria and Italy, and whose Swiss German-, Romansch- and Italian-speakers live scattered among a hundred and fifty valleys. Their cuisine shows influences from both neighbouring countries: polenta, pasta, risotto and osso buco co-exist peacefully with dumpling-like dishes and strudels. Graubunden being one of the foremost hunting cantons, venison, chamois and even marmot feature regularly. Bündner wines (especially those of the Herrschaft villages) are some of the finest in Switzerland; those of neighbouring Valtellina (which in its Veltliner days used to belong to the canton) also bear investigation.

The Swiss Germans in general have a less developed 'culture of the table' than the French- or Italian-speakers. For them the whole business of food is slightly more complicated, invitations seldom spontaneous, wine drunk on special occasions rather than routinely. Powerful soups precede pork dishes with cabbage (fresh and salted). Fish has recently become fashionable, but lamb has a hard time competing and seems to be regarded as food for *Gastarbeiter* ('guest workers', like Turks, Greeks and Brits). Sausages are legion, potatoes are practically *de rigueur*. Probably

Eastern influences in canton Graubunden.

most representative of all is the wonderful *Rösti* (page 76), a sort of grated potato pancake seen as the quintessential Swiss-German dish by the French speakers. (The dish has even given its name to the river Sarine, otherwise jokingly referred to as the *Rösti-graben*, the deep dividing 'ditch' between French- and German-speaking Switzerland.) Supper in Swiss-German homes will often feature a vegetable or fruit pie (*Wähe*) served with *Milchkaffee*. Bircher-müesli is a perennial favourite, served not as a breakfast dish but as a meal in itself (lunch or supper) with fresh apple juice or milky coffee and a hunk of good bread. Wines are grown throughout German-speaking Switzerland, mainly for local consumption. In good years they can be excellent; in lesser vintages, unkind fellow confederates (usually from the more sunblest wine-growing cantons) will recommened them for the preparation of fondue; that way, no lemon juice need be added. Beers, often locally brewed, are excellent.

The French speakers of Switzerland, known by themselves as *les Suisses romands* and by the Swiss-Germans as *die Welschen* (meaning, literally, celtic – non-alemannic – and therefore foreign), are inevitably more influenced by the French culture of the table, not only from their proximity to France, but also for historical reasons – not for nothing are they descended from the Burgundians. Some of Switzerland's largest lakes are in the French-speaking part, and lake fish is frequently served – in a recent opinion poll, *filets de perches* (fried fillets of perch) was voted the most popular dish of *Suisse romande*, way ahead of that other well-known French-Swiss dish fondue, and other supposed favourites. All the French-speaking cantons (with the exception of the recently formed Jura) are wine producers and wine plays a big part in their gastronomy – as essential accompaniment, or cooked into dishes. In addition both the Valais and the Vaud are big orchard and market garden areas.

The people of Ticino, though Italian by nature, are Swiss to their fingertips and would be mortally offended if anyone suggested otherwise. Their relaxed attitude to eating and drinking, however, is thoroughly Italian and their cooking largely derived from that of Lombardy and Piemonte. Nowadays the food is almost indistinguishable from that of northern Italy, with a few delicacies such as *torta di pane* (page 45) and *mortadella e lenticchie* standing out as authentically *ticinese*. The prosperity of today's Ticino tables is, however, of recent date, for the area was somehow passed by in the tourist boom of the nineteenth century, and has only recently been opened to tourism – principally by Germans and Swiss-Germans, who value the combination of its Italian climate and atmosphere with its Swiss order and peacefulness, not to mention its delicious food and wines. In the last century, however, Ticino fare would typically have consisted of soup, cereals (barley, millet and rye), meat three or four times a year, chestnuts and dishes made from chestnut flour, rough local wine made from American and hybrid grapes, and liberal shots of local grappa, a clear grape brandy not to be confused with the Italian spirit of the same name. Polenta made from maize (corn) dates only from the 1800s; previously, it was more likely to have been prepared from millet or from buckwheat (*polenta negra*). Of even more recent date are those other 'typically *ticinese* dishes' such as risotto, noodles, gnocchi and ravioli; even potatoes took longer than in the rest of Switzerland to take root down here.

One thing that seems to unite all Swiss is their shared passion for salads, cheese and good bread – and in case this sounds too dauntingly healthy, they are also champions in chocolate consumption (though they like to share the blame for the figures with all those resident and visiting foreigners – around sixteen per cent of the population of Switzerland is non-native). Fast food has made inroads here as elsewhere – MacDonalds now have the

Beautiful
painted houses
in the tiny town
of Appenzell.

dining car concession on the train from Basle to Geneva – while at the other end of the scale, the excesses (or rather paucities) of *nouvelle cuisine* have also taken their toll. Somewhere between the two – perhaps provoked by them both – there is a return to the roots of Swiss cooking all over the Confederation, a hankering after old tastes and dishes, a need to get back to base – whatever that might be.

Switzerland is a special place. As John Hillaby commented in his foreword to *Ancient Pathways in the Alps**, 'unless they are mendicants or mad, people do not wander about in the Alps unless they enjoy it and know what to look for.' Mendicancy might be viewed askance in Switzerland nowadays, and even a certain degree of unconventionality is regarded with some suspicion. For those, however, who enjoy good food and wine and who may plan to wander about the country, this book should help them to know what to look for and where to find it. A rich gastronomic tradition has evolved on either side of the Alps over seven centuries of co-habitation by people from four distinct linguistic groups, two main religions and twenty-three different cantons. It is waiting to be discovered, far from the ski slopes and the tourist traps.

Therwil, Switzerland

*Ancient Pathways in the Alps, Giovanni Caselli & Keith Sugden, George Philip & Son Ltd., London 1988

FEASTING AND FASTING THROUGHOUT THE YEAR

'All too often', reads a brochure on popular customs and festivals in Switzerland published by the tourist office, 'we form an impression of a country by that which meets the eye. This impression may well be a pleasant one, but it contains no notion of the people, their mannerisms, beliefs, history, customs and roots which lie behind the scenes we witness. . . . We want visitors to be not just "tourists" but true guests who sample our food and our folklore, our history and our traditions.' On the surface, Switzerland, with its breathtaking scenery and apple-pie ordered villages, certainly gives a delightful impression; dig deeper, however, sample some special holiday dishes, or participate in one of the many festivals which punctuate the Swiss year, and you will be treating yourself not only to some wonderful foods, but also to a lesson in the folklore, history and traditions of the country.

In the old days the year began with ritual gifts of rich breads and moulded biscuits (cookies), typically exchanged between friends, or given by godparents to godchildren, or donated to the poor. The godparental versions often contained a token coin. Even today, no New Year's Day would be complete for the Bernese without the plumply plaited, shiny golden *Züpfe* (page 41). The fish, an ancient symbol of renewal, was also much in

Colourful musicians beat the cold at
Lucerne's classic carnival.

Festive *Züpfe* for New Year's Day.

gingerbread (*Lebkuchen*) was no longer good enough for these demanding and discerning visitors, so an elaborate variation was created which added candied peel and ground nuts to the honied and already lavishly spiced dough.

To this day, there is heated debate and stiff rivalry between Basle households each claiming to have the best recipe. Stiff also is the dough for these wonderfully chewy spiced biscuits (cookies); so much so that in the last century, cooks would be seen scurrying up to the station to hire a porter for the arduous stirring. Nowadays the electric mixer makes a good job, but for those reluctant (or unable) to make them at home, there are several shops in town from which the famous biscuits are despatched world-wide, throughout the year. The people of Zurich have their own luridly coloured *Züri-Leckerli* for New Year, as well as small sausages of quince paste and intricately moulded biscuits (cookies) called *Tirggeli* – all of which can still be found between Christmas and New Year in the Café Schober in the old part of town known as the Niederdorf.

evidence on January 1, sometimes in the form of a yeast bread, or made from more elaborate ingredients: a spiced honey dough with a gingerbread and candied peel filling from Nidwalden in central Switzerland, for instance, or a puff pastry version filled with apples and raisins from Thurgau, or yet another from the Rhine valley with a filling of ground hazelnuts, dried fruits and honey.

Fine Basle families would usher in the New Year with visits to the neighbours armed with baskets of *Leckerli* (honey and spice biscuits) and plenty of *Hypokras*, a combination of red and white wines, spices, sugar and cloves brewed up into a sort of mulled wine. Whether Hippocrates ever indulged in such a potion is not clear, but doubtless the vaguely medicinal connotations of the name made everyone feel better about drinking it. *Leckerli* (the word has gourmet/sweet-toothed overtones) date from the time of the Council of Basle in the mid-fifteenth century when the city played host to fine churchmen from far and wide. Tradition has it that the ordinary

The sixth of January marked, in pagan times, the end of the twelve *Rauchnächte*, the dark and gloomy nights when the spirits walked abroad. The Christian calendar later diplomatically adopted the date for Epiphany, and some sort of commemorative loaf incorporating a good luck charm made its appearance. The winner of the charm would chalk up the initials C M B over the door, signifying simultaneously *Christus mansionem benedict* (Christ bless this house) and Caspar, Melchior and Balthasar – and incidentally ensuring protection for the house from the evil spirits. Though the concept of a celebratory cake at this time is thus an ancient one, the actual form of today's *Dreikönigskuchen* or *Gâteau des Rois* – a plump ring of sweet yeasty buns inside one of which still lurks a good luck charm – dates only from 1952 when the custom was revived by the baking federation. Whoever gets the piece containing the talisman (formerly an almond, today more likely a plastic monarch) wins the right to wear the golden paper crown and to be king for the day.

The period between Epiphany and the beginning of Lent is a time for some really single-minded feasting, when a series of wondrously rich and stupendously fattening deep-fried pastries make their appearance in a seemingly unending range of shapes and sizes. In Lucerne, *Schmutziger Donnerstag* ('fatty Thursday', the week before Lent begins) signals the arrival of *Zigerchröpfli* (turnovers) and *Zigerchugeli* (blobs) filled with a particularly delectable soft cheese, cinnamon and hazelnut paste, deep-fried and sprinkled with cinnamon sugar. Basle bakers make a speciality of the savoury (salt) diamond-shaped, cumin-speckled *Fastewähe*, while in almost all corners of Switzerland fragile, rippling, sugar-sprinkled fritters known as *merveilles* or *Fasnachtskiechli* are consumed by the ton. Down in Ticino, *ravioli di carnavale* are not – as you might expect – pasta parcels, but featherlight pastries filled with a piquant prune purée. None of them are things you would make yourself; but purchased still warm over the baker's counter and eaten 'on the hoof' as you wander around the streets of any carnival town, they taste just right.

Herr Thüring's *Drei Königskuchen* for an Epiphany treat.

Besides many regional specialities, there are also specific carnivalesque events in which food plays an important part. Shrove Tuesday, for instance, is celebrated in Ticino with a series of street feasts, formerly for the benefit of the poor of the villages and towns but nowadays a light-hearted opportunity for locals and visitors to get together and tuck in. Most commonly on the menu is a deep yellow saffron-flavoured risotto and the local sausages known as *luganighe*. Sometimes, however, cauldrons of bubbling *busecca* (tripe) take the place of risotto, or huge dishes of macaroni, or a rich beef stew with pasta. Many of the larger towns (Lugano, Locarno, Ascona, Bellinzona)

21

celebrate in this way in the run-up to Lent, but the smaller villages provide more local colour. In Ponte Tresa, right on the border with Italy, I watched as the local policeman lent a hand with the setting up of the rough trestle tables in the *Piazza della Dogana* and from well before midday the line of expectant risotto-eaters began to build up. To one side of the square, a group of 'cooks' – painters, dairymen and builders in everyday life, but risotto champions every *Martedi Grasso* – attended in pairs to the serious business of softening the onions, frying the Arborio rice, adding the wine and the precious saffron, and finally the all-important stock, brewed up the day before from beef bones, herbs and vegetables and wheeled along in milk churns. To others fell the job of cooking festoons of short, fat *luganiga* sausages. An old lady hovered around with her tin can, ready to take home any spare supplies for supper. At last it was ready, everyone received a plate of steaming rice, sausage and a bun, adjourned to the table, adjusted the paper napkin, poured out wine and commenced the feast.

While most carnival activities take place in the period preceding Ash Wednesday, in Basle the serious business is yet to come: since the Reformation this staunchly Protestant city has always celebrated its famous *Fasnacht* one week into Lent. Some claim that this was a bit of protestant snook-cocking at the timing of what was perceived to be principally a papist fast; others, more prosaically, that the Baslers had simply failed to take into account the change from the Julian to the Gregorian calendar. (Whatever the real reason, the

celebration of carnival after the beginning of Lent has given rise to a nice epithet which is applied to those (few) Swiss who have trouble with time-keeping: 'he is like Old *Fasnacht*', means he is always late.)

At *Morgenstreich*, as the clock strikes four on the Monday after Ash Wednesday, all the street lights go out, the shrill pipes and the sombre drums break into a cacophony of sound, and the hauntingly beautiful lanterns set off on their wandering route through the town. After about an hour's strenuous piping and drumming, the *Cliques* down tools and dive into the nearest *Beiz* (pub) for a spot of refreshment. Food is not a big issue at *Fasnacht*; by their very nature, fasting dishes are a bit of a test. The greatest test of all is a

Risottata in winter sunshine by lake Maggiore.

dark brown, generously salted concoction known as *Gebrannte Mehlsuppe* (burnt flour soup) which belongs to *Morgenstreich* as Plum Pudding to Christmas Day. Onion tart (*Zibelewaie*), by contrast, is great *Fasnacht* fare: a rich golden ointment of onions bound with cream and eggs, confined in a crusty pastry case.

After the diverse excitements of carnival, thoughts begin to turn impatiently to the ending of winter. In Zurich in mid-April the townspeople and guilds celebrate an occasion known as *Sechseläuten* ('six bells') which climaxes as the clock strikes six in the evening, and the *Böög* (an effigy representing Old Man Winter) is set dramatically alight. On all the streets, the insistent, irresistible smell of grilled sausages fills the air, and in the cafés and bakeries there are baby *Böögs* made from various ingredients. The famous confectioners Sprüngli make a pretty irresistible version from solid chocolate gianduja coated with dark chocolate and crowned with a little snowman. This is also *Tabakrollen* time: fragile, cylindrical pastries fried to a golden brown and sprinkled with sugar. In the evening the (all-male) members of the guilds disappear for dinner into their beautiful old guild houses to either side of the River Limmat, doubtless to tuck into a plate of *Züri-Gschnätzlets mit Rösti*, the town's most famous dish of diced veal in a creamy mushroom sauce served with a golden, crusty potato cake.

Easter is a time when many neighbouring (and yet farther-flung) influences are felt in Switzerland: from eastern Europe comes the custom of elaborately decorated eggs, still painstakingly done at home by patient Swiss mums and eager children, using natural dyes made from onion skins, tea, nettles, wood shavings, saffron or cumin seed; motifs are formed from herbs and tiny leaves. The breakfast table will often be decorated with a cloth, mats and napkins specially made for the occasion. On it (besides some beautifully moulded chocolate eggs and Easter bunnies) will be served a variety of Easter breads made from a buttery dough similar to that for *Züpfe*: nests, wreaths, doves or hares ready for dunking into hot chocolate or coffee, or dipping into the runny yolk of the Easter morning egg. Later in the day there may be lamb, kid or rabbit: all favourite treats for Easter Sunday lunch in Ticino and in Suisse romande. The Swiss-Germans, for their part, indulge for dessert in a wondrous tart called *Osterfladen*, the best versions of which contain masses of almonds, eggs, sugar and dried fruits baked inside a fragile pastry crust.

Summer is the time for a mass movement of cows, goats and people up to the high pastures, and a number of cheese-related traditions are explored in the dairy chapter (page 47). The most important summer festivity, however, is Swiss National Day on August 1. On this day in 1291 the three forest cantons (Uri, Schwyz and Unterwalden) formed their alliance, from which developed the Confederation of modern-day Switzerland. Bakers all over the country stock little quartered buns, each with a Swiss cross patriotically superimposed and sometimes a flag stuck jauntily on top; barbecues are lit and the evening air is thick with the smell of grilled

Würste, *saucisses* and *salsiccie* of all sorts; beacons are lit high in the mountains and in prominent positions in even the tiniest hamlet or village; fireworks explode far into the night.

Late August was traditionally the time for the Emmentaler harvest thanksgiving meal known as *Sichlete*, an annual event for all those who had helped to bring in the harvest. On the wood-fired stove there were bubbling pots of fragrant, yellow, saffron-flavoured lamb stew; on the dresser a home-cured ham, sausages, slabs of bacon, salt pork, beans from the garden and the indispensable *Züpfe* (braided bread). For dessert there were meringues – which in the Emmental have always assumed dimensions undreamed of in any other part of the world – billowing blowsily from beneath a swirling load of whipped cream. To drink, there was white and red wine from neighbouring canton, Vaud, and plenty of home-distilled apple *Schnapps* known as *Bätziwasser*. As farming families diminish in size, and gas-guzzling combine harvesters supersede the hordes of hungry helpers, huge *Sichlete* meals are fast fading from Emmentaler memories. Marlis Hofer, a farmer's wife from Schleumen near Burgdorf reports reassuringly, however, that nowadays two or three small villages will often combine forces for a joint harvest thanksgiving.

In a similar vein to the *Sichlete* festivities is *La Bénichon* from Fribourg, originally a church dedication anniversary celebration, but latterly a sort of harvest thanksgiving. A friend from the area describes (with evident nostalgia for lost childhood days) the typical programme: breakfast brought a *cuchaule*, a saffron loaf resembling a giant golden-brown pine cone,

spread with butter and a sweet mustard pickle known as *la moutarde de Bénichon*. For lunch there was a broth in which a ham and vegetables had slowly simmered, followed by the ham itself with cabbages and potatoes. Then came a rolled shoulder of mutton with mashed potatoes and a unique dish known as *poires à botzi*, a sort of compote of caramelized pears served in accompaniment. Essential also was the home-grown salad of escarole, sown with forethought in July for the September feast. Once again there were mountains of meringues for dessert, with whipped cream, coffee and *beignets de Bénichon*, the same wafer-thin, sugar-dusted *merveilles* which are reserved in other parts of Switzerland for carnival, but which form an integral part of any *fribourgeois* festivity.

Down in the Valais there is a traditional autumn celebration meal known as *le brissolet* which consists of chestnuts (parboiled and then baked), selected cheeses from the upper Valais, grapes from the vineyards and chunks of raw smoked bacon. Chestnuts feature also in Ticino, where autumn is *castagnata* time; out come the trestle tables once more, chestnuts are roasted in huge ovens and consumed with a *tazzin* or two of local Merlot. Now is also the time of the year for fairs, large and small, among the best known of which are the *Comptoir Suisse* in Lausanne and the Basle Autumn Fair – five hundred and twenty years old in 1990 and one of the oldest in Switzerland. Once again, the smell of *Klöpfer* (cervelas) fills the air, teeth are sunk into toffee apples, *Rosenkiechli* (waffles) sizzle on the stoves and *Mässmöcke* (boiled sweets),

Magebrot (a spicy chocolate loaf) and *Lebkuchen* (gingerbread) are everywhere on sale. The *Chäschuechli* stand on the Petersplatz, manned by arch-specialists Heidi and Freddy Koschara, is famous throughout Basle. Each year the couple take two weeks 'holiday' from their jobs (hers at a butcher's shop, his with one of the chemical companies) to turn out unimaginable numbers of piping hot cheese pies made from Freddy's home-made puff pastry and an exquisite filling of eggs, cheese, cream and milk.

Another early November market is the *Rüebli-Märt* held in Aarau, capital of the carrot-growing canton of Aargau. Even if the idea of a cake made of carrots sounds a dubious one, try it: all that is left of the vegetable is its sweetness and moisture, which combined with a good quantity of hazelnuts and eggs gives a cake which is one of Switzerland's best. Later

it's the turn of onions when the town of Bern celebrates the *Zibelemärit*, originally the culmination of a two-week Martinmas market, but now held on one day only and devoted almost exclusively to onions. Tradition has it that when the city burned down in 1405, the market gardeners from neighbouring villages and towns came to the rescue and helped put out the fire. In gratitude to them, they were entitled thereafter to sell their onions in Bern on the last Monday in November each year. The trainloads of visitors who annually descend on the city do not come in search of mere onions for the stock pot: here, the bulbs are plaited and beribboned, fashioned into puppet shapes or little witches mounted on broomsticks, made into beautiful table decorations or door hangers. Purchases complete, you can with some relief (for it always seems to be bitterly cold on this late-November

Chestnuts pop . . . and *Rosenkiechli* sizzle at the Basle autumn fair.

Monday) allow yourself to be seduced inside one of the bustling *Beize* (simple, bistro-type places) or restaurants, from out of whose doors waft tantalizing smells of soups, sausages and onion tart.

In the build-up towards Christmas, December 6 looms large in the calendar – particularly if it's a child's Advent calendar, often home-made to an original design or carefully constructed at nursery school. From early morning on the sixth, the bakeries are full of sweet little yeasty St Nicholas figures, with rakish hats and scarves and twinkling curranty eyes and buttons. As night falls, the tinkling of a distant bell is heard and down the street comes St Nicholas dressed in his traditional Santa Claus costume and pulling a barrow full of treats. He is accompanied by the slightly sinister *Schmutzli* clad from head to foot in black, and bearing a list of all the children's names. They file up and, on hearing their name called, recite a little poem (and/or confess to transgressions committed during the past year.) For their performance they each receive a small sack of fruit, nuts and sweets.

When December 11 comes around, the people of Calvin's sober city of Geneva (which has a rather meagre tally of holidays and festivals) seize the chance to celebrate *L'Escalade* with understandable gusto. The Mère Royaume's heroic behaviour in repelling the invading Savoyards in 1602 by pouring over them a vat of boiling soup is immortalized in the quantities of *soupè de la Mère Royaume* poured down receptive throats at this time. In time-honoured tradition the town's pastry cooks and confectioners rise to the occasion, in this case with variously-sized chocolate soup pots filled with an array of marzipan vegetables.

As Christmas approaches, baking activity reaches fever pitch. The huge variety of baked goods to be found at this time of year – the pear breads from Lucerne, Glarus and Graubunden, the ubiquitous St Nicholas figures, the Bernese deep-fried pastries, the spiced and honied *Biberli* from Appenzell, the inevitable *Lebkuchen*, and the whole, marvellous range of *Weihnachtsguetzli* (Christmas biscuits (cookies)) – were all originally designed to relieve the meatless tedium of the Advent fast. On Christmas Eve the feasting begins again. Modern-day Switzerland, as you might expect of a country with such a variety of languages, cultures, religions and climates, has no single, 'typical' Christmas menu. In the German-speaking part, the ham (or smoked pork shoulder) tradition lives on, in Geneva there may be more of a French influence, while over by the Italian border is the Ticino a dish from Lombardy or Piemonte may feature, with *panettone*, a light brioche-type bread for dessert. An increasingly popular solution in many homes is *fondue bourguignonne*, which gives the grateful cook a chance to join in the festivities.

On New Year's Eve the skiers in mountain villages snake their way down the mountainside in torchlit processions, while the townspeople make their way towards the cathedral square, bottles tucked under their arm, to hear the bells ring out the old year. Champagne corks start popping, the Glühwein gets brewing. Another year has passed.

ZÜRI-GSCHNÄTZLETS

Diced Veal with Cream and Mushrooms

SERVES 4–6

600g/1¼lb tender boneless veal, diced
200g/7oz veal kidneys, trimmed and diced
flour
salt and pepper
50g/2oz/4 tbsp butter
1 onion, chopped
200g/7oz mushrooms, sliced
juice of ½ lemon
200ml/7fl oz white wine
200ml/7fl oz cream
chopped parsley

Though nowadays this famous Swiss dish most often consists only of veal and mushrooms in a creamy sauce, originally kidneys were also included. Skip them if you prefer, and increase the veal to compensate. The dish is traditionally served with *Rösti* (page 76), though pasta is permissible.

Dust the veal and the kidneys in seasoned flour and fry in small batches in the butter in a heavy frying pan. Remove as they are ready and keep them warm.

Fry the onion gently until soft.

Add the mushrooms and lemon juice, cover and cook gently for about 5 minutes until the juices run. Remove the lid and cook hard to evaporate juices.

Add the wine and allow to reduce to almost nothing. Add the cream and simmer steadily for about 5 minutes.

Return the veal and kidneys briefly to the pan to warm through. Check seasoning, sprinkle with parsley and serve at once.

ZIBELEWAIE

Onion Tart

SERVES 6

1kg/2¼lb onions
25g/1oz/2 tbsp butter
salt and pepper
300g/10oz shortcrust (basic pie)
*   pastry*
3 eggs
200ml/7fl oz cream
200ml/7fl oz milk
optional: 50g/2oz streaky bacon
*   cubes*

This is a favourite throughout German-speaking Switzerland whether for a restorative breakfast at *Fasnacht* in Basle, for a warming lunch after the *Zibelemärit* (onion market) in Berne, or for supper in Schaffhausen.

Slice the onions finely. Stew them gently in a covered pan with the butter, salt and plenty of black pepper for about 30 minutes until golden and tender. Heat the oven to 200°C/400°F/Gas Mark 6.

Roll out the pastry to fit a 30 cm/12 inch quiche pan. Whisk together the eggs, cream, milk, and salt and pepper to taste. Spread the cooked, cooled onions in the pastry case, pour over the egg mixture and scatter the bacon on top (if using).

Bake the tart for about 35 minutes or until set and golden brown.

TICINESE CARNIVAL RISOTTO

SERVES 4–6

1 onion, chopped
1 clove garlic, crushed
2 tbsp oil
300g/10oz/1⅓ cups round-grain
*   rice*
200ml/7fl oz red wine
250ml/8fl oz dry white wine
450–500ml/15–16fl oz stock
2 pinches of powdered saffron
salt and pepper

Made with risotto rice (Arborio or Vialone), red and white wine, saffron and the best stock you can muster, this makes a wonderfully robust and tasty supper dish. Serve with good pork sausages.

Soften the onion and garlic in the oil without allowing them to take colour. Stir in the rice and cook for a few minutes. Moisten with the wine and cook, stirring, until it has completely evaporated.

Heat the stock and dissolve the saffron in it. Add it gradually to the rice, still stirring. Season to taste. As each addition is absorbed, add a little more.

Continue to cook for 15–20 minutes or until the rice is just *al dente* but still quite soupy.

ÄMMITALER SCHÖFIGS

Saffron Lamb Stew from the Emmental

SERVES 4

1kg/2¼ lb boned shoulder of lamb
salt and pepper
25g/1oz/2 tbsp butter or 1 tbsp oil
1 litre/1¾ pints/4 cups water or
*   stock*
a pinch of saffron
1 onion
2 cloves
1 tbsp flour
2–3 tbsp dry white wine

A gaudy and delicious lamb stew, this used to be served at the harvest thanksgiving meal as a starter to precede a ham with all its accoutrements, but nowadays is more often served as a main dish. Be sure to bake, borrow or steal a rich, yellow *Züpfe* (page 41) for mopping up the juices, and serve with buttery mashed potatoes.

Trim the lamb and cut into bite-sized pieces. Season and toss in hot butter or oil until lightly browned. Moisten with the water or stock mixed with the saffron.
 Add the onion stuck with the cloves and simmer for about 1 hour or until fork-tender.
 Mix the flour with the wine to a smooth paste. Stir into the stew and simmer for 15 minutes more.

CHÄS-CHÜECHLI/RAMEQUINS AU FROMAGE

Cheese Pies

MAKES 12 PIES EACH 10 CM/4 INCHES DIAMETER

250g/8oz shortcrust (basic pie) or
*   puff pastry*
250g/8oz Swiss cheeses, grated
200ml/7fl oz cream
300ml/10fl oz milk
2 tbsp flour
3 eggs
salt and pepper
grated nutmeg

Typical Swiss fast food, these little pies are served at fairs and festivities throughout the year. Use a mixture of well-matured Swiss cheese (e.g. Gruyère, Sbrinz, Emmental).

Heat the oven to 200°C/400°F/Gas Mark 6. Roll out the pastry and line buttered foil moulds 10 cm/4 inches diameter*. Sprinkle the cheese into the tartlet moulds.
 Whisk together the cream, milk, flour, eggs, salt, pepper and nutmeg. Divide the custard between the moulds.
 Bake at once for about 20 minutes or until golden brown and beautifully risen. Serve immediately as they sink rather fast.
 (*For one large pie, use a 28 cm/11 inch quiche pan and bake for about 30 minutes.)

OSTERFLADEN

Easter Tart

SERVES 8

*50g/2oz white bread, sliced
(2 medium slices)*

milk to cover

2 eggs, separated

*125g/4oz/1⅓ cups coarsely ground
almonds*

125g/4oz/10 tbsp sugar

*50g/2oz/⅓ cup sultanas (golden
raisins)*

50g/2oz/⅓ cup raisins

flour

375ml/13fl oz cream

250g/8oz puff pastry

Some *Osterfladen* contain ground rice, cornflour (cornstarch), fécule or even semolina; this one, from an old handwritten Basle family recipe book, uses up stale bread or milk rolls, mixes them with almonds, fruit, cream and eggs, and encases the whole mass in light pastry.

Remove crusts from bread and soak in milk. Squeeze out excess milk and discard. Mix the bread in a large bowl with the egg yolks, almonds and sugar.

Rinse the dried fruit, pat it dry and toss it in flour. Add to the mixture.

Whip the cream into soft peaks. Beat the egg whites until stiff but still creamy. Fold both into the mixture.

Heat the oven to 180°C/350°F/Gas Mark 4. Roll out the pastry thinly and line a lightly buttered 30 cm/12 inch quiche pan.

Pour in the mixture and bake for (sic) 'five-quarters of an hour'.

SILVIA'S BASLER BRUNSLI

Chocolate and Almond Christmas Cookies

MAKES 20–30,
DEPENDING ON SIZE

*100g/3½oz plain (semisweet)
chocolate*

250g/8oz/1¼ cups sugar

250g/8oz/3 cups ground almonds

2 tbsp flour

2 tbsp cocoa powder

½ tsp ground cinnamon

2 egg whites

a pinch of salt

2 tbsp Kirsch

sugar for sprinkling

Brunsli, almond-laden dark chocolate mouthfuls with gooey middles, are special to Basle, and are one of the very best of all the many Christmas cookies. There are countless recipes; this one, from a former neighbour, is a winner.

Melt the chocolate in a bowl over hot water. Mix together in a large bowl the sugar, almonds, flour, cocoa powder and cinnamon.

Beat the egg whites with the salt until stiff but still creamy. Fold them into the dry ingredients. Add the melted chocolate and Kirsch. The dough should be quite

firm and should clean itself off the sides of the bowl.

Sprinkle the working surface with sugar and roll out the dough at least 1 cm/¹/₂ inch thick. Cut shapes with cookie cutters and place them on a baking sheet lined with non-stick baking parchment.

Leave to dry out for at least 4 hours (otherwise they will collapse on baking).

Heat the oven to 250°C/475°F/Gas Mark 9. Bake for 5 minutes. The cookies keep well for at least a month in an airtight tin.

RÜEBLI-TORTE

Carrot Cake

A good carrot cake should be damp and nutty, with a sharp lemony icing for contrast. This one, from a Swiss friend, is particularly good. Swiss confectioners sell marzipan carrots to put on top. The cake is best made at least one day ahead.

Heat the oven to 180°C/350°F/Gas Mark 4. Cut a disc of non-stick baking parchment to fit a 26 cm/10 inch spring-form cake pan. Butter and flour the sides.

Beat together the egg yolks and half the sugar until thick and pale. Grate the carrots finely and mix them in with the ground nuts, lemon juice and zest. Sift together the flour and baking powder and fold in also.

Beat the egg whites with the salt to soft peaks; add the remaining sugar and continue beating till stiff. Fold into the cake mixture.

Pour into the prepared pan and bake for about 50 minutes or until just firm. Release cake from springform and spread with warmed jam. Mix together icing (confectioners') sugar and lemon juice and spread on top.

SERVES 6–8

5 eggs, separated
250g/8oz/1¹/₄ cups sugar
250g/8oz carrots
250g/8oz/3 cups ground almonds
grated zest and juice of 1 lemon
75g/2¹/₂oz/¹/₂ cup flour
2 tsp baking powder
a pinch of salt
3 tbsp sieved apricot jam
250g/8oz/2 cups icing
    (confectioners') sugar
2–3 tbsp lemon juice

31

DAILY BREAD

'Bread', claimed an article in the London *Daily Telegraph* a few years ago, 'is an emotive substance. Shortage of it has traditionally been a sign of dangerous irritation among those prone to riot.' It's tempting to suppose that one of the reasons why the peaceable Swiss have always shown so little in the way of riotous tendencies is to be found in all those gorgeous breads they bake and consume. Certainly anyone who suffers from dangerous irritation at the sight of serried ranks of plastic-wrapped 'white sliced' – known in Switzerland, to my eternal chagrin, as *Englisches Toastbrot* – will be in their element here: white, brown, long, round, crown-shaped or marked with a cross,

the warm, wheaten, crusty loaves crowd the shelves and are completely irresistible to all but those of the sternest resolve.

Sampling the wares of local bakeries is an excellent way to get to know what each region has to offer and adds a whole new dimension to travels (and doubtless also to travellers) around Switzerland. The six million-odd lucky inhabitants of this tiny, intensely bread-conscious country have at their disposal some three thousand small bakeries, plus about fifty in-house bakeries owned by the two main supermarket chains. A typical village such as ours (with about four thousand inhabitants) has two private bakeries and a supermarket

A selection of cantonal breads specially
baked at the Maison du Blé et du Pain,
Echallens. (Clockwise, from top right: Jura,
Zurich, Neuchâtel, Valais, Basle, Ticino,
Geneva. Vaud is in the centre)

with a double delivery of still-warm loaves each day. Between these three outlets, there is a choice (even allowing for some overlap) of about twenty-five different varieties, whose ranks on high days and holidays will be swelled by special festival breads. Little wonder that expatriate Swiss suffer severe withdrawal symptoms when they move abroad.

Generalizing rather, you could say that the German-speaking Swiss prefer darker loaves of some substance, while the French- and Italian-speakers favour fragile-crusted, light white breads. Virtually every canton has its own: Basle's is an extremely well crusted, waisted loaf characterized by its high water content, chewy texture and huge holes. It is made from unbleached white flour from (mainly) locally grown soft wheats with a proportion of hard wheat for good body; sometimes a little light brown flour known as *Ruchmehl* or *farine bise* is also included. Zurich bread has been described (probably by a Basler) as 'rather austere, like its inhabitants'. It is a wide, stubby loaf made also from unbleached or brown flour, whose regular oval shape makes it especially valued as a hotel restaurant bread where easily-cut, even slices are required. Farther east, the bread from St Gallen (its shape shared by Appenzell and Thurgau) is a rounded, dumpy loaf with a pendulous 'nose'. Like the English cottage loaf, it has the reputation of making particular demands on the baker's skill and is made either from unbleached or light brown flour.

In central Switzerland, the bread from Schwyz, one of the three original forest states of the Confederation, bears a remark-

able resemblance to a British policeman's truncheon. It comes into its own at carnival when numerous loaves are festooned from the broomstick brandished by the *Blätz* (carnival clown). It would be reasonable to assume that the breads of the two tiny half-cantons which make up Unterwalden in the very heart of Switzerland would be the same. In fact, though made of a similar dough, they are fundamentally different in shape, one round, stout and crusty, the other long, soft and sylphlike.

Country chef Andreas Putzi at work on his farmer bread for the Restaurant Farnsburg, Ormalingen, near Basle.

In Graubunden, 'the canton of a hundred and fifty valleys' where rye is extensively grown (and generously subsidized), bread is often made on a 'sponge' or leaven system from at least two-thirds rye and one-third wholewheat flour. In Poschiavo, the loaf is called *Bratschadella* and is delicately and deliciously flavoured with aniseed. Its characteristic ring shape enables it to be suspended on special rods (safe from the nibblings of the house mouse), where it will keep for anything from a week to a month.

The dense, dark, flat Valaisan rye bread (sometimes incorporating walnuts) is an interesting one: also made on a leaven system to increase its keeping qualities, in the old days it was made once a year in huge quantities to last for a season, and baked in the communal oven (*le four banal*). So stiff and unmanageable was the dough, and so voluminous the quantities, that the whole business was traditionally regarded as men's work. Another special bread – its recipe a closely guarded secret of village baker Herr Zuber – can be found in the village of Mund, high above Brig in the upper Valais. Here in the steeply sloping meadows (interplanted with rye which acts as a mulch) can be found the prized *Crocus sativus*, the saffron crocus. In the Middle Ages the village was renowned for its saffron cultivation, doubtless a legacy of returning or itinerant crusaders. By the turn of this century the crocus had all but disappeared, but recently, with encouragement from the local priest, some smallholders decided to revive the culture. In 1989 the magnificent total of one kilo (about two pounds) of the priceless spice was harvested.

A special wedding bread in an Emmental bakery.

Fribourg bread is made from equal quantities of unbleached white, brown and rye flours; it is round, fairly flat and marked off into small, bun-like squares which can easily be broken off. From Neuchâtel comes the wonderfully rich, brioche-like *taillaule*, usually reserved for a Sunday treat. In neighbouring Vaud, the loaves are white, crusty and signed with a cross, while in Geneva a baguette-style dough is used, shaped into a round, flat loaf, liberally floured and marked into lozenges. The most recent addition to the catalogue of cantonal breads was created by the bakers of canton Jura, which only obtained its independence from Bern in 1975: the Jurassien bishop's crozier is proudly and pointedly emblazoned on its floury crust.

Pane reale, the bread of Ticino, is widely available in other parts of Switzerland under the guise of *Tessinerbrot* or *pain tessinois*. *Ticinese* bakers, however, manage to make theirs uniquely light with an eggshell crust. As the loaf travels north through the Gotthard it gathers weight and acquires a more substantial crust – still delicious, but subtly different. The *pane della Valle Maggia*, on the other hand, is difficult to find outside the area, so pounce on it when you find it and enjoy it while you may: round and rather flattened, it is made from a blend of white, wholewheat and rye flours and has a soft, floury crust and crumb, big holes and a wonderful flavour.

With such a basketful of breads to choose from, you might think that few people would bother to bake at home. Yet the Swiss house-wife, bound as she often is to the home by a mixture of convention and highly irregular school timetables, has plenty of time for leisurely bread-baking and an apparently natural ability for the task. In all the supermarkets and bakeries there is a brisk turnover of fresh and instant-blending dry yeast, along with many specially packaged flours and blends. Immense – and justifiable – pride is taken in the skilful tressing of a plaited milk loaf (*Zopf* or *Züpfe*), while the smell of new-baked *Burebrot* ('farmer bread') is no stranger to country kitchens.

The tradition of baking in wood-fired ovens also lives on. The one housed in the spruce and beautifully-equipped church hall kitchen of our village is stoked up regularly by a group of enthusiasts who buy a special mix of flours from Herr Staub (the dusty miller), roll up

their sleeves, work up the dough, knead away their tensions or bad temper, and turn out a batch of loaves for the family and the freezer. Some country chefs, such as Andreas Putzi at the Restaurant Farnsburg above Ormalingen near Basle, make a feature of their home-baked bread, crusty and dusty from the ashes on the bottom of the oven.

The area best known for its rich, buttery, plaited milk loaves is the Emmental, where a *Zopf* becomes a *Züpfe* and is almost obligatory at the Sunday morning breakfast table. Invited to the Emmental to take instruction, I turned up one Saturday bake-day in the tiny hamlet of Schleumen near Burgdorf, home of the Hofer family. A bundle of firewood crackled merrily in the bread oven outside the grand old farmhouse, under whose expansive roof were housed (on various levels and in various compartments) the young farmer and his family, plus twenty cows, a hundred-odd pigs, stacks of wood chips for the central heating and bundles of sticks for bread baking, sundry farm machinery and several farm cats. Upstairs in the kitchen of the adjacent *Stöckli* or granny annexe, Marlis Hofer, my instructor for the day, was preparing the ingredients for two sorts of bread.

First we made the dough for the *Burebrot* ('farmer bread'). Into a big washing-up bowl went four kilos of light brown flour, salt and several cooked, peeled, grated potatoes sur-plus to yesterday's *Rösti*. 'Not essential', explained Marlis, 'but they do make the bread good and moist.' Next came a mixture of milk and water into which the yeast had been smoothly stirred. I rolled up my sleeves and

A typical farmhouse in the Emmental.

went to work. Occasionally Marlis would peer over my shoulder, pinch the dough experimentally and indicate that more kneading was required. She showed me the special Emmentaler way of kneading called '*Ährekneten*', the idea being to grasp fistfuls of dough all down its length between thumb and middle finger, using alternately right and left hands, squeezing hard and, at the same time, lifting to aerate. When she'd finished, a clear pattern resembling an ear of wheat ('*Ähre*') remained; I went valiantly through the motions, then stood back expectantly awaiting the expert's comments. 'It takes a bit of practice,' she said after a pause, in an encouraging sort of voice.

From downstairs, husband Hansueli called to say that the wood was burnt through and the oven hot. We descended, Marlis raked out the dying embers and reached inside fearlessly (the temperature was still over three hundred degrees Celsius) to brush out the ash; the door was left open to reduce the temperature to the required two hundred-degree mark. Meanwhile we shaped the loaves ready for baking. The soft dough was divided up into eight or nine pieces with a plastic dough scraper and a small piece set aside for a *Speckkueche* (bacon tart), Hansueli's favourite food: '*eine Kalorienbombe!*' he grinned with evident relish, cheerfully casting aside any cares for his cholesterol count. For the loaves, each piece of dough was squashed flat, the edges folded up and into the centre, inverted and rolled around to a plump ball. The small piece reserved for the '*Kalorienbombe*' was thinly rolled out and anointed with cream and scattered with diced

bacon. The loaves were lined up on a lightly floured plank and we set off downstairs again. Then each one was lifted on to the baker's peel, slashed with a sharp knife and shunted onto the oven flour, closely followed by the *Kalorienbombe*.

Finally it was the turn of the *Züpfe*, made of finest white flour, salt, sweet Emmentaler butter, fresh yeast and full cream milk. Marlis stressed the importance of thorough kneading to distribute the gluten and give the correctly 'threaded' *Züpfe* texture. She worked her way up and down the dough with her knuckles like a practised physiotherapist proceeding up and down her patient's spinal column. Once well-risen, the dough was knocked down, cut into two pieces and each one rolled out under damp palms to a long, smooth rope. Plaiting with three strands is child's play, she explained, but the resulting braid is somewhat flat; plaiting with only two strands is definitely moving into the advanced class, but only thus do you get a fine, upstanding, three-dimensional braid.

Emmentaler housewives must be born with an inbuilt ability to plait two-stranded *Züpfe*. Or perhaps it comes from watching Granny from a tender age, coupled with constant practice. They certainly don't learn it from books, and Marlis looked sceptical when I mentioned brightly that I planned to try and describe the process on paper. I watched her lay the silky ropes of dough in front of her on the table in the form of a large 'x'. Using both hands, she repeatedly lifted and crossed the strands of dough with deft, rhythmical movements, wove the whole into a plump plait and tucked the ends under. 'Got it?' she asked, rather breathlessly, and – I thought – a mite optimistically. Not only could I not describe it, it was far from certain that I could even do it myself. I was put to practise with two tightly rolled-up, crossed-over tea towels on the kitchen table while Hansueli watched, hugely amused, from the doorway. After several abortive attempts ending in a mass of mangled linen, quite suddenly the penny dropped; it was a bit like learning to ride a bike (and I couldn't describe that on paper either).

When both loaves were ready, their crusty bottoms tested for the correctly hollow sound, Marlis thrust one of each into our willing arms. On the way home, we made a pit stop at the village *Käserei* (dairy) and bought a hunk of well-matured Emmentaler made from unpasteurized milk. From the cheese and the *Züpfe*, which shared the same soothing smell of warm cows and new-mown hay, we made a meal the like of which has seldom been had.

Finally, when any of these beautiful breads begins to stale, the old finger-wagging proverb '*Brot vergeuden ist eine Sunde*' ('to waste bread is a sin') comes as a timely reminder of the great respect in which bread has always been held in Switzerland – not to mention the famous Swiss sense of economy. Recipes abound whose sole purpose in life is to accommodate stale bread, ranging from cheesy bread-and-butter puddings to cherry cakes, as well as others with bizarre names such as *Fotzelschnitten* ('raggedy slices'), *Vogelheu* ('bird's hay') and *Alte Mäa* ('old man').

The time-honoured Emmental tradition of plaiting *Züpfe*. Plenty of practice is required before the penny drops.

BUREBROT/PAIN PAYSAN

Farmer Bread

MAKES 1 LARGE LOAF

400g/14oz/2²/₃ cups plain white (all-purpose) flour
150g/5oz/1¹/₄ cups wholewheat flour
150g/5oz/1¹/₂ cups rye flour
1 tbsp salt
25g/1oz fresh yeast, or 2 tsp easy-blend (quick-rise) dry yeast
250ml/8fl oz warm water
about 200ml/7fl oz buttermilk, sour milk or plain yogurt

In Switzerland you can buy a special combination flour for this 'farmer's loaf' which includes white, wholewheat, rye and spelt flours. The proposed mix comes close, and the addition of buttermilk (or alternatives) gives a wonderfully moist and chewy bread.

Mix together the flours and salt. Crumble or sprinkle in the yeast.

Add the water and buttermilk (or alternatives) and knead well by hand, or in an electric mixer with dough hook fitted, to a fairly firm dough which does not stick excessively to the hands or bowl.

Allow to rise at room temperature until doubled in bulk. Knock down the dough and shape into a ball. Drape a tea-towel into a basket or bowl a bit bigger than the dough and flour it generously.

Put in the dough and leave to rise again for about 30 minutes.

Heat the oven to 220°C/425°F/Gas Mark 7. Invert the loaf on to a baking sheet. Make a lattice of cuts on the loaf's surface, 1 cm/¹/₂ inch deep, using a sharp knife. Bake the loaf for 40–45 minutes or until crusty.

Farmer bread fresh from the oven.

ZÜPFE

Plaited Milk Loaf

SERVES 4–6 PEOPLE

500g/1lb 2oz/4 cups strong white
bread flour
1½ tsp salt
1 tsp easy-blend (quick-rise) dry
yeast, or 15g/½oz fresh yeast
60–75g/2–2½oz/4–5 tbsp soft
butter
about 300ml/10fl oz milk
1 egg, beaten

Definitely an advanced piece of baking, but one which will give you much satisfaction. Because the dough is intricately shaped and the loaf baked free-standing, it is important to use a strong bread flour. For best results, allow the dough to rise overnight in the refrigerator; this makes it easier to plait.

Mix together the flour, salt and dry yeast. (If using fresh yeast, add it later as instructed.)

Cut the butter into pieces and work it into the flour as if making pastry.

Warm the milk to blood heat (whisk in fresh yeast at this point if using) and add to the flour.

Knead vigorously by hand (about 10 minutes) or in an electric mixer (about 5 minutes) until smooth and springy and the dough starts to clean itself off your hands (or off the sides of the bowl). Add sprinkles of flour if needed to achieve this.

Cover the bowl with a plastic bag and leave the dough to rise until doubled in bulk (about 1½ hours at room temperature, or overnight in the refrigerator).

Knock the dough down, cut into pieces, flatten each piece and roll up tightly to a sausage. Then roll out each sausage under slightly dampened hands to a rope about 60 cm/2 feet long.

Lay the ropes of dough on a large working surface as in diagram and plait (braid) as shown on page 39.

Put on a baking sheet lined with non-stick baking parchment and leave for about 15 minutes.

Heat the oven to 200°C/400°F/Gas Mark 6. Daub loaf liberally with beaten egg and wait 5 minutes. Daub again, then bake for about 45 minutes or until golden brown and hollow-sounding when tapped on the base.

PAIN DE SEIGLE

Rye Bread

MAKES 1 ROUND, FLAT
LOAF

*100g/3¹/₂oz/1 cup wholewheat
    flour*
*150g/5oz/1¹/₂ cups coarsely ground
    rye flour*
*400g/14oz/3 cups finely ground rye
    flour*
2 tsp salt
*25g/1oz fresh yeast, or 2 tsp easy-
    blend (quick-rise) dry yeast*
about 450ml/15fl oz warm water
2 tbsp chopped walnuts

A dense and delicious loaf from the Valais, made of rye and wholewheat flours and walnuts. The loaf should be kept for a day or two before using and cut into very thin slices; it will hold for at least a week.

Mix together the flours, salt and fresh or dry yeast. Add enough water to give a very stiff and sticky dough, more like a stiff cake batter than a bread dough. Knead very thoroughly and leave to rise at room temperature until doubled in bulk (at least 2 hours). Knock down and work in the walnuts.

Flatten it out to a disc, fold the edges into the middle, invert and roll round to a ball. Put on a baking sheet and leave to rise again for about half an hour.

Heat the oven to 200°C/400°F/Gas Mark 6 and bake the loaf for about 1 hour or until hollow-sounding when tapped on the base.

VOGELHEU/EIERRÖSTI

Bread Omelette

SERVES 2 HUNGRY
STUDENTS FOR SUPPER

*150g/5oz bread (about 6 medium
    slices)*
2 tbsp oil
4 eggs
salt and pepper
200ml/7fl oz milk
2 tbsp chopped chives
*optional: cubed leftover cooked meat
    or ham*

This cheerful recipe also rejoices in the name of *Studenten-futter* (student fodder). It's a sort of bedsit bread omelette with herbs and (if you're feeling really reckless) a little leftover meat.

Cut the bread into cubes and fry in hot oil in a non-stick pan until golden.

Mix together the eggs, salt, pepper, milk and chives (and meat or ham cubes if used). Pour mixture into the pan and cook until set.

Invert it on to a lid or plate, slide it back into the pan and cook the other side.

Rye Bread

RAMEQUIN

Cheesy Bread Pudding

SERVES 2

6 slices of good bread
2–3 tbsp dry white wine
100g/3½oz Gruyère cheese, grated
150ml/5fl oz milk
100ml/3½fl oz cream
salt and pepper
2 eggs

This savoury bread pudding from Fribourg bakes to a rich, bubbling golden brown. Serve with salad for supper.

Butter an ovenproof dish and put in bread slices. Sprinkle with wine.

Heat the oven to 200°C/400°F/Gas Mark 6.

Mix together the cheese, milk, cream, seasoning and eggs. Pour the custard over the bread and bake for 20–25 minutes until golden brown.

PARTYBROT

Party Bread

A speciality of Swiss-German bakers: bun-sized pieces of dough are arranged in a quiche pan and baked. The bread comes to the table and everyone breaks off a roll. Make up any of the doughs in this chapter (or one of your own choosing) and allow it to rise once in the bowl until doubled in bulk. Knock down and divide into pieces, each weighing 25–50g/1–2oz depending on the size of rolls wished (during baking they will approximately double in size). Shape by rolling them around under cupped hands on an unfloured board or marble slab, then place fairly close together in a lightly greased quiche pan or shallow baking dish. Allow to rise again for about 30 minutes. Spray with water and sprinkle if wished with poppy seeds, sesame seeds, fine oatmeal etc. Bake in a heated oven 220°C/425°F/Gas Mark 7 for 30–35 minutes or until golden brown and hollow-sounding when tapped on the base.

ANDREAS PUTZI'S FARNSBURG BUREBROT

Andreas Putzi's Farmer Bread

Herr Putzi's honey-coloured loaves are made from flours milled locally from four different grains, deliciously speckled with wheatgerm and crushed rye. They are baked in the wood-fired oven built into the kitchen wall of the restaurant. Try, at the very least, to find an unbleached white flour, and a coarsely milled wholewheat.

Mix together the flours and salt. Crumble or sprinkle in the yeast. Mix in enough water to make a rather slack dough. Knead well. Allow to rise in bowl until doubled in bulk (1½–2 hours).

MAKES 1 LARGE OR
2 SMALL LOAVES

800g/1¾lb/5⅓ cups plain white
   flour
100g/3½oz/1 cup wholewheat
   flour
1 tbsp salt
25g/1oz fresh yeast, or 2 tsp easy-
   blend (quick-rise) dry yeast
about 500ml/16fl oz warm water

44

Knock down to a flat disc, fold edges up into centre and press them down firmly. Invert dough (seams under) and roll round to a plump cushion. Leave on a floured board for about 30 minutes. The dough will spread out rather.

Lift on to a floured baking sheet, slash four or five times with a sharp knife, sprinkle lavishly with flour and leave for a few minutes.

Heat oven to 220°C/425°F/Gas Mark 7. Bake for about 40 minutes or until pale golden.

TORTA DI PANE

Bread Pudding with Chocolate and Raisins

SERVES 8

250g/8oz stale bread (about 11 medium slices)
1 litre/1¾ pints/4 cups milk
1 vanilla pod (vanilla bean), split, or 1 tsp vanilla essence (extract)
3 eggs
1 tsp salt
150g/5oz/¾ cup sugar
50g/2oz plain (semisweet) chocolate, grated, or 2 tbsp cocoa powder
75g/2½oz/½ cup raisins
optional: a small glass of grappa
75g/2½oz/¾ cup pine nuts

A typical Tessiner family pudding made from stale bread steeped in milk, mixed with raisins, spices, chocolate, eggs, spiked with a shot of *grappa* (grape brandy) and topped with pine nuts.

Break up the bread and put in a bowl. Boil the milk with the vanilla and leave to infuse for a few minutes. Remove the pod (bean), if used, and pour the milk over the bread. Leave for 3–4 hours or overnight.

Reduce to a smooth purée in a food processor or vegetable mill.

Beat together the eggs, salt and sugar until light and fluffy. Add to the bread mixture, with the grated chocolate or cocoa powder, raisins and grappa, if using.

Heat the oven to 180°C/350°F/Gas Mark 4. Pour mixture into a shallow buttered ovenproof dish, scatter pine nuts on top and bake for 1–1¼ hours or until set.

Torta di pane keeps well for several days in the refrigerator, covered with foil.

OF COWS AND CHEESE

The best way to get a feel for the importance of the dairy industry in Switzerland is to visit the village dairy shop. In the early hours before opening time, the farmers wheel along their churns of warm milk, either for collection by a cooperative or for cheese-making in the adjoining dairy. At about 7.30 a.m. the doors are open for business. A sprightly housewife coasts by on her ancient bike, disappears inside to fill up a small pail with fresh raw milk, hangs it over the handle bars and pedals off home again.

Mid-morning, quite young children sporting luminous orange triangles (for greater visibility on their frequent walks to and from school during the day) drop in for a snack of yogurt (every conceivable flavour) or a thirst-quenching yogurt drink. The soft cheeses called quarks, of varying degrees of fatness, flavoured or natural, are purchased – perhaps destined for a wonderful Swiss cake or tart. There are Petits Suisses, cottage cheese, cream cheese, processed cheese triangles for snacks and sandwiches. Butter is seldom salted and decoratively wrapped; best for frying *Rösti* are the tubs of clarified butter. For the accompanying dish of diced veal in a creamy mushroom sauce there is a dazzling choice of rich creams, while the light *Kaffeerahm* is used to smooth and enrich the strong Swiss coffee.

Cows standing guard over the Gotthard Pass.

Over at the cheese counter, a smiling assistant in an embroidered blue smock volunteers cheeses for a fondue mixture: the customer watches as a selection of well-aged Emmental and Gruyère are freshly grated for her, and a small amount of the melting Vacherin Fribourgeois is carefully cubed. Another customer announces a raclette party at home, buys a half wheel of cheese and borrows the shop's special grill too at no extra cost. Finally the secretary of the village gym club appears to pick up a cheese platter specially ordered for their annual get-together. It is a work of art, about fourteen different sorts of cheese cut into neat portions, garnished with grapes, walnuts and tomatoes, and stuck with miniature Swiss flags.

The dairy industry is important not only at village level; it is a vital part of the whole Swiss agricultural picture – and undeniably good for tourism, too, since Switzerland without cows would be a bit like New York without skyscrapers. Approximately half the cows to be seen in pastures throughout the countryside are the dun-coloured Swiss browns; the other half (brown and white) are Simmentals. The occasional black and white Holstein also hoves into view, while in the Valais are to be found a few of the small, black Hérens breed, better known for their belligerence than for their milk yields. About a third of all the milk produced by Swiss cows goes to the dairies to be made into the myriad milk by-products upon which the country thrives. Not much is wasted: the whey goes to fatten the pigs, even milk serum is used to make a fizzy drink called Rivella. It is said to be Very Good For You.

Probably the most significant by-product of all, certainly the most complex and interesting, is cheese.

Centuries ago, cheese-making in Switzerland was confined to the mountains. Such was already the reputation of Swiss cheeses that they were used for barter. With the opening of the Gotthard Pass in the thirteenth century, alpine cheese-makers would journey to Italy to exchange their wares for spices, wine, rice or chestnuts. The tradition of barter was still thriving in the eighteenth century; contemporary records show that cheese was traded for linen, fustian, coffee and tobacco – all of which were presumably of more use than cash to the cowherd up on his alp. Until the nineteenth century the precious flat lands of the valleys had been reserved for wheat growing. Only when the potato plant began to complement bread as a staple food could lowland areas be released for dairy farming. Cheese-making extended down into the plains.

Swiss cheeses do not enjoy a system of *Appellation Contrôlée*, as is the case for some twenty-seven cheeses in France. This means that you could, if you wished, make Emmental in Évreux, Gruyère in Granada and Appenzeller almost anywhere. To be sure that you are getting Real Swiss Cheese, therefore, look for the name SWITZERLAND radiating enthusiastically out all over the crust. Alternatively the rind may be stamped with a rectangular label. A cowherd complete with skull cap, smock, clogs and alphorn is depicted standing on a precipice carved from a quartered wheel of cheese, flanked on all sides by *Suisse, Schweiz, Svizzera* and *Switzerland*.

Biggest and best known of the hard cheeses of Switzerland is the hugely holey Emmental, a mild-mannered cheese often included in a selection as a contrast to offset the more powerful varieties. It was first mentioned in despatches in 1542 though doubtless it existed long before. Its most magnificent (and unexpected) manifestation is in the form of the Cheese Express, a bright yellow dining car belonging to the Swiss Railways and run by the Swiss Cheese Union. Resembling a vast horizontal slab of Emmentaler complete with *trompe l'oeil* holes, it trundles daily through the Swiss countryside on the route between Basle and Brig. On board you can sample a selection of freshly cut Swiss cheeses and specialities such as fondue, raclette and toasted cheese open sandwiches.

To watch Emmental being made, you have only to arrange to be in almost any village dairy in the Emmental at about 7 a.m. The dairyman, always glad of a captive audience, welcomes you in his white boots and spacesuit; you could eat off the floor and the air is full of soothing childhood smells of rich warm milk. Once the cheeses have been formed,

Racks of the finest Gruyère slowly maturing in Monsieur Dougoud's cellar

the full, nutty wonder of the Emmental bouquet develops. If you like your cheeses full-flavoured, ask for well-aged Emmentals.

Gruyère is Emmental's baby brother, less than half the size and with correspondingly smaller holes; what it lacks in size, it amply makes up for in flavour. If you were under the impression that Gruyère was Gruyère wherever it grew, then a visit to Monsieur Dougoud's *fromagerie* in the attractive market town of Bulle in canton Fribourg is advised. His are serious cheeses. They bear about as much resemblance to plastic-wrapped supermarket offerings as the euphemistically-named 'chocolate cake covering' does to a bar of Lindt Excellence. Monsieur Dougoud sells five different sorts of Gruyère, ranging from mild to *extra vieux*. His *gruyère d'alpage* comes from cows which graze in summer pastures high up near the picturesque village of the same name. It spends between one-and-a-half and two years quietly maturing in the cool damp cellars below the shop. The famous Basle chef Hans Stucki likes to use it for an off-duty fondue, mixed in equal proportions with Emmental and a Vacherin Fribourgeois.

There are few hard and fast rules for fondue – at least none that are unanimously agreed upon. Sometimes equal quantities of Gruyère and Emmental are used, sometimes half Vacherin Fribourgeois and half Gruyère; or there may be several Gruyères of differing ages. A nicely federalistic *fondue quatre cantons* might contain Gruyère, mountain cheese from the Valais, Vacherin Fribourgeois and Appenzeller. There's even a version from the Tessin known as *fonduta*, made from various cheeses,

they are first put below the dairy in a rather warm cellar, to ensure formation of the famous holes. (The Italians, it seems, like big holes; the French and the Swiss prefer them more discreet. The Americans, if they had their way, would eliminate the holes and make the cheese square, a move being firmly resisted by the Emmental dairyman.) Later, during the coolly conducted maturing process – which may take anything from a month to a year –

The elegant
church of
Gruyère.

further enriched with eggs and milk and poured over either polenta or potatoes.

Then there is the business of the booze: wine, as in most of the French-speaking cantons? Or cider, as in apple-growing Appenzell and Thurgau? Or maybe not at all, as can sometimes happen in canton Fribourg. A little cornflour (cornstarch) is needed to knit things together. A shot of Kirsch, or other locally brewed spirit, is said to aid digestion of this

dish which, it must be admitted, puts a considerable strain on the system. And finally, the pan must be wide, shallow, and made of earthenware or enamelled cast iron; a fondue bourguignonne pan will not do. Almost endless variations can be played on the fondue theme; you can make up your own mixture using two or three different sorts of hard and semi-hard, well-aged cheese, allowing between 150 and 200g/5–7oz per person.

Moving the cattle along, high on a mountain pass.

Fondue should be stirred not only during the heating but also (using forks speared with bread) throughout the eating process, to avoid the risk of it curdling and/or burning on the bottom of the pan. If it curdles (recognizable when a layer of milky liquid forms on top and a layer of chewing gum below), it should be removed to the privacy of the kitchen and beaten like mad over gentle heat. If this doesn't work, a bit more cornflour (cornstarch) mixed with some wine and stirred in should do the trick. As the fondue nears its conclusion, there should be a delicious golden crust in the bottom of the pan, known sometimes as *la croûte*, or more reverently as *la religieuse*. This can be gently prised off and awarded to honoured guests who understand the wonder of such things. Some people gently scramble in an egg or two at this point.

Swiss-Germans frequently prescribe peppermint tea with fondue; they fear that a cold drink on top of melted cheese may provoke horrible happenings in their insides. The Suisses romands have no such qualms and enjoy a glass (or three) of wine with fondue, and sometimes a *coup du milieu* (small glass of Kirsch) as well. Afterwards, little is required but a light fruit salad or fresh fruit.

Sbrinz, Switerland's answer to Parmesan, probably originated in Brienz, near Interlaken. The fact that it was referred to by Pliny simply as *caseus helveticus* ('Swiss cheese') suggests that in Roman times it was the only one available. It was certainly exported in considerable quantities as long ago as the sixteenth century to Italy, a market which continues to flourish today. True Sbrinz connoisseurs hack chunks from the whole cheese with a special weapon resembling an oyster opener. The chunks are then crumbled (never cut), and eaten with a slab of smoked bacon or air-dried meat, hunks of good bread and a glass of fresh apple juice or a home-brewed *Schnapps*. Because it is so hard, dry and intensely flavoured, Sbrinz is ideal for cooking: it never goes stringy and little is needed for a good cheesy flavour.

A curiosity is the tiny, castle-like Schabziger (sapsago) from canton Glarus with an intense flavour which makes it ideal for grating over background dishes like pasta, potatoes or rice. It vies with Sbrinz for the label of 'the oldest Swiss cheese'; certainly its composition (skimmed milk with added buttermilk and a powerful herb named *Melilotus coerulea*) and its *Stöckli* (conical) shape have remained unchanged for the past five hundred years. As recently as twenty years ago, the *Schabzigermändle* ('sapsago man') was a regular visitor to country areas: about once a month he would do the rounds of the villages selling his conical wares from house to house. On the menu that evening would be sapsago grated over freshly boiled potatoes (*Gschwellti*).

The people of Appenzell are known for their piquant sense of humour, as well as for their excellent semi-hard cheeses, favoured by 'mountain men and monks for the last seven hundred years'. Some Appenzeller cheeses are gently creamy, others are almost alarmingly assertive. The most pungent version is called *Räss*, a cheese before which even devotees of Munster, Epoisses or Limburger have been known to quail. Its penetrating smell is due to its being brushed regularly during the long ripening process with a special brine made with the addition of white wine, plenty of pepper and an arcane mixture of herbs and spices. Although produced all year round, it is especially popular in the autumn when it is served with another seasonal speciality: new (still-fermenting) wine. One foggy November day while visiting the toy town of Appenzell, I went in search of a *Räss*. When the lady behind the cheese counter asked if I would like my purchase wrapped in a smell-proof package, I assumed that this was evidence of the fabled Appenzell sense of humour. I laughed obligingly. She gave me a knowing look. The cheese disappeared into a back parlour and re-emerged neatly vacuum-packed. '*Schöne Reise!*' ('have a nice journey!'), she beamed.

When I got it home and released it from its package, it was clear that not only did the lady have a sense of humour, she had also shown immense consideration for my fellow travellers. Like many strong-smelling cheeses, however, its bark turned out to be worse than its bite. It had been recommended for either a salad or a fondue, but Herr Heeb, chef at the Hotel Säntis, suggested an even better home for it: grated over a crusty, bacon-speckled potato cake for a memorable *Appezöller Rösti*.

A selection of Tilsiters, Goat's cheese, Emmental (with big holes), Gruyère (with the little ones) and Schabziger (in the centre).

in their skins, Tilsiter is cut in fingers, and each are dipped in turn into the dressings.

One of the nicest members of the cheese board is the dumpy, cylindrical Tête de Moine or Bellelay, which originated in the monastery of the same name in the Swiss Jura. The cheese is halved horizontally and speared in a central spindle, to which is attached a rotating blade. As the blade is rotated over the cut surface, a tonsure-like portion of cheese results. (It would be nice to think that the name Tête de Moine is in some way related to the way the cheese is cut, but the cheese is centuries older than the rather modern device used to cut the slices.) Another 'monastery' cheese is the already-mentioned Vacherin Fribourgeois, almost always used in fondue, but excellent in salads and with vegetables. It came originally from Montserrat in Catalonia where it was known as *caseus vacarinus*. A homesick Swiss friar is said to have made his way back to Fribourg some time in the thirteenth century with the secrets of its fabrication, and it has been made in Switzerland ever since.

From Thurgau, the rolling farmland and orchard canton to the south of lake Constance comes Tilsiter, third in importance after Emmental and Gruyère. It is a medium-sized, creamy, semi-hard cheese whose manufacturing secrets were brought to this corner of Switzerland from Tilsit in east Prussia (now Sowjetsk) by two prodigal farming sons, Wegmuller and Wartmann, in 1893. It comes in three strengths: green (made from pasteurized milk) is mild; red (made from raw milk, sold abroad as Royalp) has more character; gold is a full-cream Tilsiter, richest of all. In Thurgau there exists a cosy communal meal known as *Stupfete*: in the middle of the table goes a bowl of onion-flavoured vinaigrette (and sometimes a soft cheese dressing too). Potatoes are boiled

Finally comes raclette cheese which has given its name to the now-famous dish. Though much appreciated in the winter months by tired and hungry skiers, it was originally a summer speciality. Years ago (so one of the stories goes) high up in his summer quarters, a herdsman in the Valais discovered and patented the best and simplest barbecue of all: the fire was lit, a wheel of cheese made on the alp was cut in half and its cut surface held close to the red hot embers. As it melted, it was scraped off ('*raclé*') and eaten with a few

Cheeses on display at Monsieur Dougoud's *fromagerie*, Bulle.

boiled potatoes and pickled vegetables brought up from the valley.

The best raclettes are still made thus, though the office of raclette scraper calls for heatproof hands, asbestos arms – and a steady supply of Fendant to keep him (or her) scraping. Electric raclette grills or grill-ovens can be hired or bought for use at home. The grill supplied by the dairy shop comes close to the original principle, only instead of the half cheese being held against the fire, it is cradled below a fierce heat; someone is then deputed to do the scraping off. With the grill-oven, everyone does their own thing and slides precut cheese portions on neat little spades under the heat until melted.

These are the hard and semi-hard cheeses which have established Switzerland's reputation as a cheese-making nation *par excellence*. Unless otherwise indicated, they are made from raw milk. The soft cheeses are another story. Usually made from pasteurized milk, they tend (with the exception of some superb goats' cheeses) to be vaguely reminiscent of soap. There was once a sensational soft cheese whose arrival on the market signalled the beginning of autumn. It was called Vacherin Mont d'Or, from the Swiss Jura, and it came confined in a small sprucewood box about the diameter of a compact disc. Inside the box, the cheese was further confined and perfumed by a band of bark. Gentle undulations in its upper

Fresh goat's cheese.

watch this symbolic opening of the short summer season. In early autumn, the process is repeated in reverse, the bells are polished up again and the slow, sonorous procession down to the winter quarters in the valleys begins once more. The fruits of these summer months are the *Alp-* or *Bergkäse, fromages des alpes* or *formaggio alpe stagionata* – medium-sized, firm, fragrant mountain cheeses with a venerable crust and a memorable flavour. In order to qualify for the name, they must be made on the alp, from raw milk, and from cows whose diet consists exclusively of lush grass, wild flowers, dandelions and clover.

High above the ski resort of Valbella in Graubunden, the cheese-maker greeted us one August morning just before seven. There are ninety-nine cows on the Stätzerhorn alp ('there were a hundred,' he explained apologetically, 'but one of them died last week of a heart attack') owned by twenty-seven different farmers from villages in the valley. They come up in mid-June, stay till mid-September and are tended and milked twice daily by two herdsmen. Every morning between 6 and 10 a.m., the cheese-maker goes to work. During the winter he is employed on the ski lift, visible from the dairy door.

Weak rays of early morning sunshine filtered through the window and lit up the burnished copper cauldron where the milk was already warmed and turned by the addition of rennet and the carefully selected starter. The radio blared out alternately *Jesu Joy of Man's Desiring* and Swiss 'knees-up' country music. While the curds were gently stirred, the cheese-maker busied himself with the supplementary

crust signalled that the time was ripe for digging in – always with a spoon, for the consistency of Vacherin was such that anything else would have invited disaster. The flavour was incomparable, evoking pine forests, sweet mountain air and rich, creamy milk. Then came listeriosis. Vacherin Mont d'Or is now made from pasteurized milk and is once more on the shelves.

Though the bulk of cheese-making is nowadays done in the lowlands, the tradition of alpine cheeses is alive and well and living – for a few summer months only – in mountain pastures from the Ticino to the Bernese Oberland. In some areas (notably around Gruyère, in the Toggenburg and in Appenzell) the ascent of cows and cowherds to their summer pastures is in itself quite a ceremony; the former are adorned with burnished bells and flowered crowns, the latter sport their best embroidered waistcoats and skull caps and all the village (as well as a good number of spectators in the better known areas) turns out to

Making alpine cheese above Valbella,
Graubünden. The curds are broken up . . .
scooped into the cheese cloth . . . The whey is
drained off . . . and the cheeses pressed.

task of kneading mounds of butter to remove excess liquid. They were then patted into shape, corseted between wooden bats, wrapped in black plastic and put in the cold room.

By now the curds in the cauldron resembled cottage cheese granules swimming about in a watery liquid. After a quick check with the thermometer, he took a piece of cheesecloth the size of a headscarf, anchored two corners nearest him between his teeth and rolled the far edge of the cloth once or twice over a bendy metal strip to make a sort of fishing net. Balancing his stomach on the edge of the cauldron, his feet clear off the ground, he leaned in and scooped up as much curd as would fit in the cloth. Then he rocked himself back on to his feet and with great skill transferred the corners of the cloth from teeth and metal strip into one hand. Holding the bag of curds high, like an inverted balloon, he allowed the whey to drain off. The whole bundle was pressed into a plastic, porous, straight-sided mould and a weight went on top. He leant heavily on it, then left it to its own devices while he continued the process with the remaining curds in the cauldron.

Later, all the cloths were removed and the 'cheeses' (already surprisingly compact and firm) were turned and left for their twenty-four hour rest. Next day, he would consign them to the salt bath for a further twenty-four hours. Then begins the long ripening process. At the end of the summer, they are distributed proportionately amongst the farmers whose cows have grazed on the alp. Up at Valbella this seems to be a relatively private affair; in the Justistal near Sigriswil in the Bernese Oberland, however, this process (known as *Chästeilet*, the dividing up of cheeses) is a colourful and joyful festivity which draws together farmers, cowherds, families, friends and spectators from near and far. The cheeses are piled up in lots, each one corresponding to the output of a certain cow during the whole summer. Later, by a complicated but scrupulously equitable system, the cheeses are allotted to each of the assembled farmers.

Any cheeses not distributed in this way will be sold on to dairy shops and specialists all over the country. For a guided tour of mountain cheeses (and a quick geography lesson of the Swiss alps thrown in), a visit to the tiny cheese shop Glauser in Basle is a must. Hidden away in the old part of town on a steep, narrow street called Spalenberg, it is owned and run by the Egli family. Herr Egli establishes and nurtures the all-important contacts with the alpine dairymen, while Frau Egli and her superbly versed staff are responsible for sales. Perhaps the ultimate cheese shop is down in Lugano. You can find it – literally – by following your nose, for the aroma of the Bottega del Formaggio Gabbani on the via Pessina can be picked up several blocks away. Walls, ceilings and shelves are festooned with cheeses from near and not so near, local and imported. Lino Gabbiani, like the Eglis, has made a speciality of matured mountain cheeses: from Valle Maggia, Val Blenio, Leventina and the Val di Muggio. Some are made from cows' milk, some from goats' milk, and some from a combination of the two. He describes them as 'expensive rarities for nostalgic Tessiner connoisseurs in search of childhood memories.'

Signor Gabbiani's famous cheese shop in Lugano.

FONDUE

SERVES 4

plenty of good crusty bread
200g/7oz each of: Gruyère,
  Emmental and Vacherin
  Fribourgeois cheese
1 clove garlic
300ml/10fl oz dry white wine
juice of 1 lemon
a little grated nutmeg
2 tsp cornflour (cornstarch)
1 small glass of Kirsch
black pepper

In Switzerland, fondue is usually prepared by the man of the house; here is our man-of-the-house's version.

Cut the bread into cubes and put in a basket.

Grate the Gruyère and Emmental; cut the Vacherin into small cubes. Put all the cheese in the fondue pan with the garlic, wine, lemon juice and nutmeg.

Mix together the cornflour (cornstarch) and Kirsch and add to the pan. Bring gently to the boil, stirring assiduously. Simmer gently for 3–4 minutes.

Just before transferring to the spirit burner at table, season with freshly ground pepper.

SERVES 3–4 AS A MAIN
COURSE SUPPER DISH

1kg/2¼lb firm, waxy potatoes
salt and pepper
100g/3½oz bacon, cubed small
1–2 tbsp oil
150g/5oz Appenzeller Räss cheese,
grated

SERVES 1

3 tbsp packaged muesli with raisins
and nuts
150ml/5fl oz plain yogurt
100ml/3½fl oz/½ cup milk
4–5 tbsp orange juice
1 small apple, grated
optional: 2 tbsp honey or sugar
other fresh fruit as available

APPEZÖLLER RÖSTI

Pan-fried Potatoes with Bacon

This version of the famous cantonal dish comes from Herr Heeb of the (almost impossibly) quaint Hotel Säntis on the main square in Appenzell. Great for supper with a salad.

Cook the unpeeled potatoes in boiling salted water until barely tender. Drain and leave overnight. Then peel and grate them on a coarse cheese grater. Season them with salt and pepper.
  Fry the bacon in a heavy frying pan until the fat runs. Add more oil if needed to film the bottom of the pan. Mix in the potatoes, then press them down to form a cake.
  Cook for about 20 minutes over moderate heat until the underside is crusty and golden. Invert a plate on top of the pan and turn out the Rösti.
  Heat more oil in the pan and slide the Rösti back in to cook the other side – about another 10 minutes. Sprinkle the grated cheese on top, cover and leave for a couple of minutes to allow the cheese to melt.

BIRCHERMÜESLI

Dr Bircher-Benner's original Birchermüesli contained only oats, water, lemon juice, condensed milk, fruit and nuts. Nowadays, more dairy products are added; sometimes even huge swirls of cream are piped on top – which must somewhat upset the balance the good doctor was striving for. It is a highly nutritious calorie bomb, not so much a breakfast dish as a meal in itself, and is often enjoyed for lunch or supper with good bread and a glass of milk.

Stir together all the ingredients and let the Birchermüesli stand for about 15 minutes. Other fresh fruit may be added if wished.

ÄLPLER MAGRONE

Macaroni with Bacon, Cream and Cheese

SERVES 4

300g/10oz elbow macaroni
300g/10oz potatoes, peeled and
    cubed
150g/5oz bacon, cubed streaky
200ml/7fl oz cream
black pepper
grated nutmeg
100g/3½oz Sbrinz cheese, grated
1 onion, sliced
25g/1oz/2 tbsp butter

This recipe (from a booklet on Sbrinz by the Swiss Cheese Union) is a sort of glorified macaroni cheese with, for extra calories, potatoes, bacon cubes and cream. It is traditionally served with apple slices tossed in butter with cinnamon-sugar; a sharply dressed salad might be an alternative accompaniment.

Cook the macaroni and potatoes in boiling salted water until just tender – about 10 minutes. Drain.

Fry the bacon until lightly golden. Pour in the cream and season with pepper and nutmeg. Mix in the macaroni and potatoes.

Heat the oven to 180°C/350°F/Gas Mark 4. Layer the mixture with the grated cheese in a lightly buttered ovenproof dish. Bake until golden and bubbly (about 10 minutes).

Meanwhile, fry the onion in the butter until golden; scatter on top of the macaroni.

REAL RACLETTE

Light a good fire. Buy yourself a half wheel of real Raclette cheese, preferably from the Valais (Gomser, Bagnes, Orsières etc.), between three and five months old. Scrape off the rind, top and bottom, so that the cheese can melt more easily. Prepare boiled potatoes in their skins and have ready a supply of gherkins or cornichons, pickled onions and black pepper. When the fire has died to a mass of glowing embers, procure yourself a large stone and put it before the fire. Set the half cheese on top, its cut surface exposed to the heat. Nearby have a supply of plates. As the cheese melts, scrape it off on to a plate and serve at once. Continue in this way until everyone is full.

GROSSMUTTI'S MILCHBRATEN

Pork Braised in Milk

SERVES 6

800g/1¾lb boned spare rib (butt)
  or loin of pork, rolled and tied
2 cloves garlic
salt and pepper
oil
1 litre/1¾ pints/4 cups full cream
  milk
1 onion stuck with a clove
1 stock (bouillon) cube
1 tsp cornflour (cornstarch)

Milk products seem to find their way into many dishes in Switzerland, even a roast of pork. Here the meat is garlic-studded and cooked in milk, which combines with the meat juices to cook down to a wonderful creamy, garlicky sauce. Serve with ribbon noodles.

Stick the pork with pieces of garlic and season. Sear in a heavy roasting pan in hot oil on all sides.

Heat the oven to 180°C/350°F/Gas Mark 4. Pour the milk over the meat and add the onion and stock (bouillon) cube. Bake for 1¼–1½ hours, basting frequently with the milk and turning once or twice.

Remove the meat and let it stand for at least 20 minutes before carving.

Meanwhile, discard the onion and boil the cooking juices steadily to reduce to about a cupful. Mix some of the liquid with the cornflour (cornstarch) and whisk into the sauce. Boil up once more to thicken, stirring constantly.

CHEESE SALAD

SERVES 3–4

300g/10oz Tilsiter cheese
1 shallot, chopped
chopped chives
a bunch of radishes
salt and pepper
1 tbsp Dijon mustard
3 tbsp oil
1 tbsp vinegar
2 pinches of sugar

Typical of the northeastern part of Switzerland, this dish could also be made with Appenzeller, Vacherin Fribourgeois or Gruyère. The sharp mustardy dressing provides an essential counterpoint to the creamy richness of the cheese.

Grate the cheese or cut into matchstick strips. Mix in a dish with the shallot, chives and halved radishes.

Whisk together the remaining ingredients for the dressing, pour over and allow to infuse for about 30 minutes. Serve with boiled potatoes.

THE FEDERAL SAUSAGE FEAST

In a country like Switzerland where the purchase of a piece of meat is likely to put you in serious bother with your bank manager, it is no surprise to find a highly developed and diverse sausage industry. Here, the humble 'banger' becomes more than a breakfast dish or careless Monday night fodder; to study the window of a Swiss butcher's shop is an education in the art of the possible. You may not succeed in making the proverbial silk purse out of a sow's ear, but you can make a magnificent sausage.

The Swiss in general consume twice as much pork as beef, with the Swiss-Germans leading the field both in pig-raising and in sausage consumption. Enthusiasm for sausages in *Suisse romande* and the Tessin is a little less unbridled – though this is not to say that there aren't some wonderful indigenous *saucisses* and *salsiccie* to be found. First come the sausages which are raw and destined to remain so, such as *salami* and *salametti*, the oddly angular *Alpenklübler, Pantli and Salsiz* and – stretching the sausage point slightly – the sundry raw hams and air-dried beefs from eastern Switzerland and the Valais.

For the famous *Bündnerfleisch*, prize pieces are needed from beef hindquarters, best of all from a beast whose provenance and feeding habits are well-known to the *Bündnerfleisch*

A typical selection of sausages from the French speaking part of Switzerland. In the foreground are the horse-shoe-shaped *saucisses au chou* and *saucisses au foie*. Behind are *saucisson vaudois* for a *papet vaudois*.

man. Sometimes he is a farmer who cures meat as a sideline, more often a professional butcher. The legs are boned out and divided up following the muscle separations into three separate pieces. When the pieces have been salted and peppered, the permitted red food colouring is added and they spend at least three weeks maturing in the cool cellar. Later they go up into the attic, or out under the eaves to twist and turn slowly in the cool alpine breeze until the flavours are fully developed. By this time the meat will have lost up to half its moisture content (hence its apparently horrendous price) and is ready to be served to hungry mountain walkers or après-skiers. It is an essential component of the popular *Bündner Teller* which otherwise includes home-cured sausages, *Salsiz*, ham and bacon, and an important adjunct to the rustic *Bündner Gerstensuppe* (page 75).

Other sausages require cooking to be edible and could be termed 'boiling sausages'. One of my favourites is the deliciously robust and dumpy *saucisson vaudois*, made of pork and beef and lightly smoked. Interestingly, while most sausages are feminine (*die Wurst*; *la saucisse*, *la salsiccia*), the Vaudois version (*le saucisson*) is resolutely masculine. It seems that the reputation of this fine specimen was already firmly established in the time of early Helvetia, when the Roman centurions billeted in the area apparently considered that its consumption was conducive to all sorts of bold and mighty actions. In Switzerland, it's not only bank accounts which are numbered: the best Vaudois sausages are too, and come with a distinctive green seal, bearing canton Vaud's

impressive motto (Liberté et Patrie). (Neighbouring Geneva's *boutefas* is made of the same ingredients, and because it is packed into a particularly voluminous piece of pig's casing, its dimensions are even more impressive than that of the *saucisson*.)

Some of the sausages to be found in Ticino hailed originally from Lombardy and Emilia Romagna: the rich, gelatinous *cotechino*, for example, and *zampone*, a boned pig's foot stuffed with minced (ground) pork and other goodies. Indigenous offerings include an extremely rich pork sausage from Lugano known as *luganiga* which takes centre stage on Shrove Tuesday served with cauldrons of creamy, saffron-flavoured risotto; and *mortadella* which in Ticino is a quite different animal from Bologna's sausage of the same name. Here, it is made of pork, fat, liver and spices and though often cooked up with lentils or white beans, it is also air-dried for raw consumption, when it closely resembles salami.

In another category come all sorts of weird and wonderful cold meats (cuts) known in Swiss-German as *Uffschnitt* (correctly *Aufschnitt*, or 'cut-ups'): smooth pink pork- and veal-based confections studded with pickles, pistachios, peppercorns or pieces of tongue, and without which any self-respecting Swiss breakfast buffet would consider itself incomplete. The very up-market ones are decorated with multi-coloured lozenges, crosses, stars, blocks and circles which would look quite at home in a patchwork quilt. 'An attractive assortment of cold meats (cuts), presented artfully and imaginatively, is an expression of good will and joy in one's profession [of

butcher]', states a booklet published by the Swiss School of Butchers and Charcutiers. 'They should be the jewel in the crown of the whole range of *charcuterie* on offer.' Conveniently (since it's often difficult to make up your mind which sort to buy), they may be bought assorted: as the assistant's fork hovers over the available selection, you just point at the pieces which appeal and she makes up the required weight for you.

Then there are the sleek white sausages native to the abbey town of St Gallen, which consist principally of veal with some pork and milk to keep them looking suitably pale and interesting. They are simply wonderful thrown on the barbecue or tossed in nut-brown butter; or they can be wrapped in spinach and ham, dressed up in puff pastry, baked till golden brown and served for a semi-smart (though economical) supper. A recent addition to the range of white sausages, in deference to ever-increasing demands for 'light' charcuterie, is the chicken sausage. Where plain, coarse-cut pork sausages are concerned, each region of Switzerland seems to have its own version, whether cut in medium lengths and known as *Schweinsbratwurst*; or spiralling around a wire pyramid, sold by the metre and called *saucisse à rôtir*; or coiled, snake-like, on the Ticinese butcher's slab, stuck through with a long toothpick and denoted simply *salsiccia*.

Hams air-drying in the attic
at Churwalden, Graubünden.

The German-speakers also favour a variety of smooth pink smoked pork sausages such as the Basler *Klöpfer* (alias cervelas or summer sausage), the St Galler *Schübli(n)g* and *Stumpen*, the *Emmentaler* sausages and the ubiquitous *Frankfurterli* and *Wienerli*. Because they are already cooked, any of these can be divested of their skins and used in salads. Alternatively, they can be heated gently and served with good bread and mustard (typical Swiss fast food), or – perhaps best of all – slashed and barbecued. The Suisses romands prefer the smoked, horseshoe-shaped *saucisses au chou* and *saucisses au foie* from cantons Neuchâtel and Vaud, where the basic pork mixture is enlivened with the addition of, respectively, finely chopped cabbage or liver. As is appropriate for a wine-growing area, a little white wine also enters into the composition. Probably the most controversial sausages of the whole Confederation are *Blutwurst* (black pudding or blood sausage) and *Leberwurst* (liver sausage), which no true Ticinese (and few Suisses romands) would ever eat, but which are consumed with great relish by the Swiss-Germans.

The Swiss, not surprisingly – given such an *embarras de choix* in the matter – consume sausages (and cold meats) very frequently, with plenty of potatoes variously prepared (*Rösti*, *frites*, potato salad) and/or fried onion rings, onion sauce or apple purée. One of the better known sausage-based dishes is a *Berner Platte*, often prefixed ominously with the adjective *reichhaltig* – ample or copious. It is to

Bernese cooking as *choucroute* is to the food of Alsace – and its origins just as fiercely disputed. One version dates it from just after the French Revolution, when Switzerland became a battleground for the French against the Austrians and their allies. Though wartime provisions were scarce and ill-assorted (so legend goes), the villagers did a quick whip-round, raided larders and cellars, and between them managed to muster an impressive repast for the returning heroes: ham, bacon, Bernese tongue sausages, beef, smoked pork and pork knuckles piled up on top of a mountain of *Sauerkraut*, salted turnips, beans and potatoes. The dish became a Sunday special, and is served to this day in numerous inns throughout canton Bern and beyond.

The early autumn, recalls Madame Huguenin of the Swiss National Tourist Office (a temporary exile in Zurich but a native of Neuchâtel), when the weather is often at its best in Switzerland and the schoolchildren have their autumn holiday, is the time for residents of Neuchâtel to celebrate *La Torrée*: the picnic place selected and the fire lit, the typical rich pork sausages of the region are wrapped in newspaper and/or foil and buried in the embers along with potatoes. They emerge later, fragantly flavoured with wood smoke and wet newspaper. On neighbouring lake Biel, another sausage feast is known as *der Treberwurstfrass*, a centuries-old tradition which takes place from December to March in Ligerz. A *saucisson vaudois* is steamed in the still of the village *Schnapsbrenner* (distiller).

St Gallen, home of delicious veal sausages.

Klöpfer sizzling before the embers.

The fragrance imparted by the local *marc* to the rich smoked sausage (not to mention the quantities of *marc* which presumably need to be sampled the while) can only be guessed at.

It is in November, however, that sausage fabrication and consumption reaches something of a crescendo. The tradition of the autumn slaughter and sausage feast (known variously as *die Metzgete, la Saint Martin, la grillade, la bacharia* and *la mazza*) is an ancient one. Though by no means uniquely Swiss, it is certainly celebrated here with peculiar gusto. In some parts, it was timed to coincide with Martinmas (November 11), the last day of the farming year, on which new farmhands and servants were hired and on which rent (or tithes) were due. With the harvest in and the ploughing done, thoughts began to turn to stocking the larder for winter: potatoes, carrots, beetroot and turnips would be stored in the cellar, apples and pears were ranged on shelves or sliced ready for drying in the attic, cabbage would be salted for *sauerkraut*. Knives would be honed in readiness for the poor old pig.

Though the main objective was to set by a store of meat to last the whole winter through, there were always odd bits and pieces of the animal which could not be preserved by salting or smoking, but which nevertheless must certainly not be wasted. The more presentable (and preservable) parts of the pig were thus set aside for salting or smoking, while the humbler and more perishable portions were chopped up and neatly packaged inside the animal's own tailor-made intestines, destined for immediate consumption. Since the by-products from the slaughter of an average-sized pig amounted to a huge number of sausages, even the once-large farming families were glad of a little help from friends and neighbours, who would be invited in to share the feast. Nowadays, as the family pig becomes a thing of the past (and as the Swiss birth rate continues to plummet), the heirs to the old-established 'sausage party' tradition are increasingly the innkeepers in country villages.

Sometimes the butcher and the innkeeper will be one and the same person; otherwise this is the cue for the *Störmetzger* to make his appearance. A sort of freelance butcher with a licence to kill (pigs), his skill is not limited to the slaughter and the division of the carcass, but includes the all-important preparation, seasoning and bundling up of the unpromising-looking bits into 'tasty little bags of mystery' – to borrow André Simon's definition of sausages. First come the *Bratwürste* (pork sausages) from high-quality trimmings with a good proportion of fat to lean meat; then the *Leberwürste* (liver sausages), which

consists of various unmentionable parts of the pig, plus stale bread soaked in milk and gently stewed onions (*Zibeleschwitze*) to soften the slightly aggressive flavours of the offal (variety meats); finally come the *Blutwürste* (black pudding or blood sausages) made from the blood, milk, cream and eggs. The seasonings and spices vary from one sausage to another – and from one butcher to another. Herein lies a significant part of the *Störmetzger*'s art: he brings his own stocks of freshly ground pepper, coriander, nutmeg, cinnamon and plenty of ginger, then selects, measures and mixes them himself in proportions and combinations which remain a closely guarded secret.

While pork sausages are merely twisted into lengths with a deft flick of the butcher's wrist,

Sausages on the grill at the Basle autumn fair.

liver and blood sausages must each be tied individually. You can always tell if an inn is living up to its claim to serve genuine *Hausmetzgete* (home-butchered sausages) by the homely strings at either end of the sausages: mere shop-bought sausages (dismissed by the experts with infinite scorn as 'industrial') terminate tellingly in a metal clip. Finally it is the innkeeper's job to cook the sausages and meats, prepare all manner of accompaniments – and above all provide the unique, slightly scruffy, smoke-filled, song-singing atmosphere which is part and parcel of the *Metzgete* experience.

Up in the Ajoie region of the Jura around Porrentruy, the *Metzgete* meal is called simply *La Saint Martin* and is served any time between All Saints (November 1) and Martinmas. A *menu tout cochon* (which could be loosely translated as a 'pig-out menu'), typically starts off with a clear broth in which a piece of fresh pork has gently simmered, a slice of brawn (head cheese), followed by a serving of meat from the bouillon with salads of radish and carrot. Then comes black pudding (blood sausage), prepared up here with the addition of leeks, onions, seasonings, nutmeg, marjoram and cream and accompanied by a beetroot salad and apple purée. Still to come is a roast of pork with home-made *Spätzli* (see page 79), followed by a *choucroute* fully garnished with ham, bacon and smoked Ajoie sausages. At this point, when perhaps the most that could be expected to slip down

would be a comforting crème caramel or a soothing sorbet, in comes a rich yeast bread heavy with cream, known as a *touetsché*. Jacques Montandon in his book *Le Jura à table* adds that there is always plenty to drink, 'sobriety not being considered a virtue in Ajoie'. If the quantities of the *patron*'s home-distilled fruit brandies consumed at the conclusion to this gargantuan meal are anything to go by, Monsieur Montandon is an accurate observer of the local scene.

In the Bernese Jura around Montoz, the autumn sausage party tradition takes the form of *la grillade*, where there are slight and subtle changes once again. While pork sausages and black puddings (blood sausages) are ever present, the Suisses romands evidently scorn *Leberwurst* in favour of neat little parcels called *adriaux*: roughly the same components, but packed into caul rather than sausage casings. With all of these come three sorts of salad, apple purée and *Rösti* or noodles.

The *ticinesi* have the last word on sausages. Here, according to authors Guidicelli and Bosia in *Ticino a tavola*, *la mazza* is almost a sacred expression signifying the slaughter, the day of the feast, the feast itself and the ensuing party – which has, however, remained principally a *festa di famiglia*. The sausage inventory includes *luganighe* for grilling, *cotechine* for cooking, *mortadella* for boiling and *salami* for keeps. Accompaniments range from potatoes through to beans, lentils, chestnuts and polenta.

Making *Spätzli*. The batter is pushed backwards and forwards over the boiling water . . . The *Spätzli* float to the top indicating they are ready . . . A quick swirl to stop them sticking . . . And the *Spätzli* are then drained.

CAPUNS

Swiss Chard Rolls with Sausage in
Cream Sauce

MAKES ABOUT 16 CAPUNS
SERVING 4 AS A FIRST
COURSE, 2 AS A MAIN DISH

200g/7oz/1⅓ cups flour
salt and pepper
2 eggs
100ml/3½fl oz milk
plenty of chives, parsely and basil
1 shallot
100g/3½oz salsiz or salami
about 20 chard leaves
25g/1oz/2 tbsp butter
150ml/5fl oz stock
150ml/5fl oz cream
50g/2oz bacon, cubed
grated Parmesan cheese

Cubes of *salsiz* are incorporated into a *spätzli* batter, wrapped in Swiss chard leaves, tossed in butter and gently simmered in cream and stock.

Mix together to a smooth batter the flour, ½ tsp salt, the eggs and milk. Rest the batter for about 30 minutes.

Chop the herbs and shallot finely and add them to the batter. Finely dice the sausage and add also. Blanch the chard in boiling salted water until limp. Drain and lay them on a tea-towel.

Divide the sausage mixture between the leaves and roll up carefully. Toss the packages in hot butter in a large frying pan, turning several times. Pour over the stock and cream, season to taste, cover and simmer gently for about 15 minutes.

Toss the bacon cubes in a heavy pan until golden brown. Lift out, sprinkle them over the capuns and serve with grated cheese.

BÜNDNER GERSTENSUPPE

Pearl Barley Soup with Air-dried Beef

SERVES 8

2 onions
2 small leeks
3 carrots
a 50g/2oz piece celeriac (celery root)
25g/1oz/2 tbsp butter
150g/5oz end bits of air-dried beef
* or raw ham*
150g/5oz/3/4 cup pearl barley
2 tbsp flour
about 2 litres/3 1/2 pints/8 cups
* stock or water*
salt and pepper
2 egg yolks
250ml/8fl oz cream
chopped parsley

A robust and delicious winter soup of pearl barley with vegetables and chunks of air-dried beef or raw ham, enriched with cream and egg yolks. In Switzerland you would badger the butcher for some end pieces from a chunk of *Bündnerfleisch* or raw ham (the wafer-thin slices for eating raw are far too expensive and beautiful to put into soup). Elsewhere you could use bits of ham or pork, smoked or salted.

Chop the onions, leeks, carrots and celeriac (celery root) and soften in the butter without allowing them to brown. Add the meat and pearl barley and cook for a few minutes more.

Stir in the flour, moisten with the stock, season lightly and simmer gently for 1 1/2–2 hours or until the pearl barley is tender.

Mix the egg yolks into the cream and add them to the pan off the heat. Bring almost back to the boil, check the seasoning and sprinkle with parsley.

Serve with good bread. (The soup is, if anything, even better reheated next day.)

Hams and *Bündnerfleisch* twisting under the eaves of a house in Churwalden, Graubünden.

75

HOME-MADE PORK SAUSAGES

MAKES 8 SAUSAGES

600g/1¼lb boneless pork
200g/7oz pork fat
1½ tsp salt
black pepper
2 pinches each of ground coriander,
* nutmeg and mace and dried*
* marjoram*
4 tbsp water
about 2 metres/6 feet sausage skins
* or a piece or pork caul*
* 70×50cm/30×20 inches*

Be sure to use a fairly fat cut of pork such as shoulder or neck for making your sausages, otherwise they will turn out to be tough and dry.

Chop or process together quite finely the pork, fat and salt. Grind in plenty of pepper and sprinkle on the spices and herbs. Add the water and process again or mix well with wet hands.

Fill the sausage skins and tie at intervals; or divide the mixture into eight equal-sized pieces and tightly roll up in pieces of caul.

Grill or fry the sausages and serve with onion sauce and the traditional Rösti.

RÖSTI

SERVES 4

1kg/2¼lb firm waxy potatoes
salt and pepper
50g/2oz/4 tbsp butter
2 tsp oil

The quintessential Swiss-German dish, a bit like hash browns but crustier: boiled potatoes are skinned, grated and pan-fried till golden. Firm, waxy potatoes are essential, as is a heavy-based, preferably non-stick frying pan.

Boil the potatoes until just tender. Drain and leave overnight.

Next day, peel and grate them coarsely and season with salt and pepper. Heat half the butter and oil in a heavy frying pan and press the potatoes in to make a cake.

Cook over moderate heat for about 20 minutes or until the bottom is golden and crusty.

Invert the Rösti on to a plate. Heat the rest of the butter and oil in the pan, slide the Rösti back into the pan and cook the second side – about 10 minutes more.

A sizzling plate
of *Rösti*

ONION SAUCE

SERVES 3–4

2 onions, sliced
25g/1oz/2 tbsp butter
1 tbsp flour
250ml/8fl oz stock
250ml/8fl oz white wine
salt and pepper

If you wish, you can fry the onions in the same pan after the sausages, replace the sausages and complete the sauce around them.

Soften the onions in the butter and allow them to take a little colour. Slowly stir in the flour, add the stock and wine and season to taste. Simmer for about 30 minutes or until the sauce is thick and syrupy.

PAPET VAUDOIS

Vaud Sausages with Leeks, Cream and Potatoes

SERVES 2–3

500g/1lb 2oz leeks
1 onion, chopped
1 tbsp oil
salt and pepper
6 tbsp white wine
6 tbsp stock
2 large potatoes
1 Vaud sausage (saucisson vaudois) – about 300g/10oz
3–4 tbsp cream

An outstanding supper dish for winter consisting of creamy leeks and potatoes and the traditional Vaud smoked pork (and beef) sausage. Substitute any large, smoked boiling sausage (uncooked) for the Vaud version.

Trim, wash and slice the leeks, then soften them with the onion in the oil. Season lightly. Add the wine and stock and simmer for about 10 minutes.

Peel and dice the potatoes, add them and simmer for about 10 minutes more or until barely cooked.

Prick the sausage and sit it on top of the vegetables. Cover and simmer for about 20 minutes.

Lift out the sausage. Stir the cream into the vegetables. Slice the sausage and replace.

ADDRIOT (ADRIAUX)

Liver Patties in Caul

MAKES 10 SAUSAGE
CAKES, SERVING 2–3

1 small onion, chopped
15g/¹⁄₂oz/1 tbsp butter
250g/8oz trimmed liver
*250g/8oz belly pork (fresh pork
    side)*
*25g/1oz stale bread (1 medium
    slice) or roll*
milk or water
1 egg yolk
2 tbsp cream
salt and pepper
grated nutmeg
*a piece of pork caul about
    70×50cm/30×20 inches*
oil

These tasty liver and pork 'sausage cakes' wrapped in caul come typically from the Bernese Jura. Calf's liver is rather extravagant for such a simple dish; better perhaps to use ox or lamb's liver.

Soften the onion in the butter and set aside. Chop or process together finely the liver and pork.

Soak the bread in a little milk or water. Squeeze it out and add it to the meats with the egg yolk, cream, salt, pepper and nutmeg. Add the softened onion to the mixture.

Cut the caul into 10 pieces, each about 12 cm/5 inches square. Divide the mixture evenly between them and fold them up into neat parcels. Fry gently in a little oil till golden on all sides – about 15 minutes. Serve with apple sauce and Rösti (page 76).

SPÄTZLI, KNÖPFLI and PIZOKELS

Pasta to accompany Game

SERVES 4–6

300g/10oz/2 cups flour
200ml/7fl oz mixed milk and water
1 tsp salt
3 eggs

Spätzli ('little sparrows') and *Knöpfli* ('little buttons') are a sort of crude pasta made from a thick batter of eggs, flour, milk and water. In the Engadin there's a version called *Pizokels* made with the addition of buckwheat. The batter is extruded through a special device like a cheese grater into gently simmering water or sliced in ribbons off a board; slicing the batter off the edge of the tilted mixing bowl works well too.

Whisk or process together the flour, milk and water mixture, salt and eggs to make a rather thick batter. Let it rest for 30 minutes.

Bring a large pan of salted water to the simmer. Tilt the bowl over the pan so that the batter comes right to the lip. With a sharp knife, slice ribbons or splodges of batter into the water.

Remove with a slotted spoon as they float to the top and put in a bowl of hot water until ready to serve. Continue with the batter until all used up. Just before serving, heat the butter to a sizzle and pour it over the drained *Spätzli*.

WURSTSALAT SPEZIAL

Sausage Salad with Mustard Vinaigrette

A classic dish after which many a homesick expatriate Swiss-German has been known to hanker. All village inns have their version, all called 'special sausage salad', and all identical: sliced cervelas (also called Summer Sausage in the USA), cheese, pickles, chopped onion and a sharp, mustardy dressing which contrasts pleasingly with the richness of the dish.

Skin the sausage(s) and slice or cut into cubes or strips. Cut the cheese into cubes or strips likewise. Chop the gherkins and onion finely.

Mix together all the ingredients for the vinaigrette and pour it over the salad. Toss well to coat.

Slice the tomatoes and hard-boiled egg and arrange on top. Sprinkle with chives and chill well.

SERVES 4

*4 cervelas (Klöpfer) or 600g/1¼lb
Lyonnais sausage
100g/3½oz Gruyère or
Emmentaler cheese
2 gherkins or cornichons
1 small onion
2 tomatoes
1 hard-boiled egg
chopped chives*

*Vinaigrette:
1 tbsp mustard
salt and pepper
6 tbsp oil
3 tbsp vinegar
1 tbsp mayonnaise*

Special sausage salad, guaranteed to give any expatriate Swiss the *Heimweh* (homesickness).

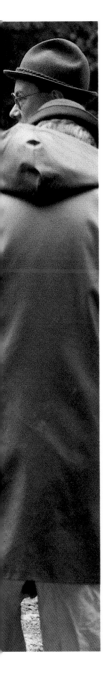

WILD BEASTS AND WILD MUSHROOMS

One of the striking things about Swiss food is the reassuring regularity with which seasonal dishes come round again each year. As the days begin to shorten, the trees to shed their reddish-gold leaves and the temperature to drop, it's time once more for game and mushrooms. On the menu in many of the small, country restaurants there may be rough terrines of wild boar or creamy, garlicky concoctions of ceps and chanterelles. Rich, rib-sticking stews (*Pfeffer* or *civets*) are perennial favourites, vying for popularity with *Schnitzels* and *Gschnätzlets* (sliced and diced game, respectively). Grandest of all is a roasted saddle of venison apparently garnished with the entire combined contents of vineyard, orchard, hedgerow and kitchen garden.

Switzerland – as befits a wild, mountainous, once-poor land – has a well-established hunting tradition. Centuries ago when game was plentiful (and often the only source of meat), the distinction was made between *Hochwild* and *Niederwild* – high game and low game. The former was the preserve of the aristocracy and included red deer, wild boar, roebuck, black grouse, capercaillie and pheasant. Also included were scavengers such as foxes, eagles – and bears. The author of the *Basler Koch-schule* (first published in 1888) admits regretfully that bear, 'in contrast to other sorts of

Members of the Jagdgesellschaft Kutzenkopf assemble one autumn morning near Liestal, Baselland.

game, is rather rare in Switzerland' – yet still sees fit to include seven recipes for cooking it, along with others for marmot, badger and squirrel. 'Low game' (young roe deer, hares and some smaller feathered fry such as partridge and snipe) was considered rather common and could thus be hunted by lesser folk.

Nowadays Swiss aristocrats (like bears) are a bit thin on the ground and the whole business of hunting has become properly democratic: rubbing shoulders with the family doctor and the forester in the local hunting association may well be the man who mends the roads. To shoot, you need to acquire a hunting permit – a fearsome process involving a year's apprenticeship learning the ropes, followed by a theoretical exam and a test of marksmanship. A steeply progressive pricing policy for 'foreigners' (i.e. anyone from outside the canton in question) helps to ensure that each community looks after its own game affairs.

Hunting in the more populous lowland cantons is quite a different kettle of fish from the wild mountain areas. In the former, hunting is let to associations whose job it is to regulate the game population of their beat throughout the year – not so much a sport, more of a gamekeeping role with a strong inbuilt conservation bias. Sometimes a member will venture out alone on a moonlit night after a wily wild boar. This is known as the *stille Jagd* ('quiet hunting'). (Wild boar, to whom the smell of maize is like the mere mention of caviar to a gourmet, are a particular menace to farmers, whose fields they thoughtlessly tear up in their quest for this delicacy.) Much more sociable and richer in colourful (and sonorous)

Waiting for the hunt to begin.

traditions are the *Gesellschaftsjagd* days ('the meets'), of which there may be half a dozen in the season. The huntsmen, clad in hunting green, assemble soon after eight on an autumn morning. Warm breath condenses in the cold morning air, hands are shaken all round, the hunting dogs quiver and whine impatiently, horns are sounded. Then after a few words of welcome by the association's president, the guns are divided into groups and allocated positions, the beaters are sent out to cover the ground.

At the end of the morning, after the picking up by dogs and beaters, lunch boxes and hip flasks come out. In the afternoon as the light

The huntsmen's
lunch break in a
forest clearing.

begins to fail, a halt is called and the day's bag is laid out on the ground: several roe deer, a few foxes, occasionally a wild boar. The horns are sounded again and the day concludes with a supper party in a hut in the wood. Sometimes the roe deer livers will be incorporated into the familiar dish of diced veal in a creamy sauce, served with plenty of golden-fried *Rösti*.

Hunting in the mountainous, game-rich areas such as the Valais and Graubunden is altogether a more fevered business – in fact it was once likened by the local doctor to a bout of malaria. It's an unwise (or unlucky) patient who chooses to be admitted to hospital during the three short weeks of the hunting season in the early autumn. An eerie quiet descends on wards, waiting rooms and operating theatres as surgeons, junior doctors and male nurses disappear *en masse* into the mountains in hot pursuit of chamois, ibex and red deer. Wives resign themselves to a period of 'hunting widowhood' punctuated by bouts of sandwich-making, laundering, cooking and thermos flask-washing. At the end of the day the victorious huntsmen make the long and arduous return journey home from the hill dragging great beasts which are then impaled on huge hooks under the overhanging roofs of the old chalets.

Swiss cookbooks include a handful of original recipes for game, though on the whole people prefer to have someone else prepare it for them and the ceremonial restaurant expedition to eat game is a well-established autumn treat. Though much of what is served in Swiss restaurants is imported (and frozen), the deeper you get into the country, and the higher into the mountains, the greater the likelihood of finding fresh, local game. In lowland areas with a mixture of dense woods and rolling arable land, roe deer and wild boar are the most likely to find their way to the chef's back door. Often he will buy the whole beast from the local hunting association and butcher it himself, reserving saddles for roasts, hind legs for steaks and medallions, shoulders for casseroles and all the other bits and pieces for savoury terrines.

In mountainous areas like the cantons of inner Switzerland, the Valais and Graubunden, chamois and red deer lead the field. To assuage the appetites of the autumn walkers there are robust gamey stews with *Spätzli* (the essential pasta-like accompaniment to game in the German-speaking parts of Switzerland) and plates of steaming red cabbage. Sometimes a leg of venison or young chamois will be marinated and roasted *en gigot*; more elderly legs will be rubbed with salt and spices and air-dried under the eaves once the weather gets cold, to be eaten thinly sliced like raw ham. Game is sometimes even used for an original fondue bourguignonne: instead of beef, tender pieces of venison are used. By the end of the year, the taste for *Wild*, *la chasse* and *la caccia* seems to be satisfied and thoughts turn once more to warming winter dishes like fondue, onion soups and one-pot meals.

Mushroom hunting is another national sport in Switzerland, practised with varying degrees of optimism depending on where you live and what you are likely to find. Wild mushrooms (like wild beasts) are happiest in the woods and mountains. Thus the areas most flush for fungi are Glarus, Graubunden, Valais, Fribourg, the whole Jura chain and – perhaps most notably – Ticino. In all of these there is a sort of rationing system in operation (maybe one kilo per person per day) in order to ensure that there are a few ceps, chanterelles and morels left for those following on behind – and for next year. Picking mushrooms is a compulsive business and it's very difficult to stop. Working your way carefully through a pine forest, you may bump into the forester who is entitled to ask you to open up your basket and show your wares. Exceeding the permitted amount (or picking on a day of rest) is punishable by a stiff fine and probable ostracism from village society.

First hopeful forays in the Basle area when we came to live here seventeen years ago produced a car bootful of wondrous specimens, yellow, green, white, brown and grey – and not one of them edible. My richest food finds turned out to be of the field and horse mushroom variety. Confident that I could tell either of these two a mile away, I once picked a clutch of what I supposed to be the real thing and bore them home. It was when I started slicing them and they turned bright saffron yellow that I began to smell a rat. Or to be more precise, carbolic acid. A quick check with the mushroom bible confirmed that they were the dreaded Yellow Stainers and that it would be unwise to proceed any further. I consigned them to the bin.

That was before I discovered the mushroom man. In most villages in Switzerland there exists a service known as the *Pilzkontrolle* or *contrôle des champignons*. If you are in any doubt about the safety of your mushrooms, you simply take them along to have them checked. In order to qualify, mushroom controllers are put through their paces on seventy different fungi, all of which must be positively identified within twenty minutes. The twelve poisonous varieties commonest in Switzerland must further be minutely described; the pass rate is a hundred per cent: there's no margin for error in the field of fungi.

Our mushroom man is a retired biology teacher who lives in a house by the wood, grows magnificent vegetables, and checks people's *Pilze*. He can tell at a glance whether the little *omelette aux champignons* I am planning will taste wonderful, or give me a mild stomach ache, or cause me a lingering death from kidney and liver failure. At his Sunday surgeries in the autumn, the queue of mushroomers stretches from his cellar door out to

Saffron milk caps.

The mushroom controller going through his paces at Basle market.

the front gate. Most are Italians (inveterate fungophiles), each bearing assorted trophies. They peer excitedly into one another's bags, baskets and boxes, exclaiming with evident respect – or as is more usual in my case, casting pitying looks – at today's pickings. Baskets are *de rigueur*, and anyone arriving with a plastic bag gets a thorough ticking off from the expert. Wild mushrooms, he explains, have a very high water content and a good crop will crush itself by its own weight in a plastic bag, resulting in a premature batch of (festering) mushroom soup before you even get home. Knives are recommended too: untrimmed mushrooms are described as grounds for

divorce. 'If I took this lot home, my wife would throw me out!' he grumbles as he patiently sorts through a load of muddy, moss-ridden mushrooms. (Once in the window of a tiny cutler's shop in the old part of Basle, I saw a special *Pilzmesser* (mushroom knife) displayed: the blade was short and curved for removing muddy feet. At the other end was a little brush for removing undesirables from the gills and caps.)

Though my Italian neighbours seem to have a facility for finding fungi even in our apparently unpromising neighbourhood, for serious mushrooms I have to go a bit farther afield. A friend who lives in the Valais told me of her amazement when she first took up residence there to hear people gathering in the local café in the evening to discuss, wide-eyed and with expansive gestures, how many kilos of ceps or chanterelles they had gleaned in a day. It seemed, she thought then, a funny thing to get excited about. Seven years later, she's hopelessly hooked, rises at five-thirty many an autumn morning, fills her kitchen cupboards with dried, pickled, powdered and pulverized mushrooms and holds her own with the best of them in the village café on September evenings. She telephoned one Sunday announcing an expedition for the following Tuesday. 'It'll be an early start', she warned, 'there's no point in going out just to find that everyone has got there first and all the best ones have gone.'

The alarm call came at five forty-five. We crawled out of bed, donned walking boots and waterproofs and set off through the village. As we passed the chalet of a well-known fellow mushroom-hunter, she nodded with satisfaction to see that all was still in darkness – he must be still in bed. Unless of course – horrid thought – he was already up on the hill. We quickened our pace. It was still dark when we reached the favoured spot. Clutching baskets and knives, we stumbled upwards, congratulating ourselves on the fact that we were the first to arrive and praying for dawn and a good catch. Soon we found some fat little ceps; the slugs – wise creatures – had been there before us, but the mushrooms were still quite good enough for slicing and drying, for later addition to a favoured risotto or pasta dish. Small finds of brown-capped russulas

(known in the Valais as *russule charbonnière*, the charcoal burner), milky-white millers, vivid yellow chanterelles, and saffron milk caps gladdened our hearts and lent a splash of colour to the fast swelling collection. Then a cry went up: at the edge of a copse, spread out in a broad swathe, was a series of soft brownish-grey mushrooms, their caps marked with upturned scales closely resembling the

Fresh ceps, equally favoured by slugs and humans.

speckled feathers of a bird's wing. '*Ailes d'épervier*', sighed Clare happily – 'buzzard's wings', which they entirely resemble. 'Wonderful for pickling, or drying and using as a seasoning', she added. We found more and more, so many that decency – coupled with a certain desire for breakfast – dictated that we head for home. We set out our treasures on the table in front of the chalet, sorted through, selected, sliced, then sat back in satisfaction. Breakfast tasted wonderful; and supper was in the bag (or rather in the basket).

Ticino is another paradise for mushroom-seekers. Driving through Agno near Lugano at around midday one morning in October I

Dino, the
Mushroom King!

glimpsed a sign announcing 'Osteria Dino: *il re dei funghi!*', The King of Mushrooms! An opportunity not to be missed. I ground to a halt, backed up, parked and entered what looked from the outside like a transport café. Inside, it was packed with *ticinese* businessmen engaged in the all-important task of selecting – or consuming – lunch. A waiter arrived and announced today's special: home-cured *salumeria* followed by *polenta e funghi*. A plate of ham, tongue, salami, bacon and tiny pickled mushrooms the size of drawing pins soon arrived, with a choice of crusty white or rye bread.

Waiting for the main course, I studied the *Corriere del Ticino* to improve my Italian and discovered that a certain Signora Edera Ceppi from nearby Mendrisio had found, the previous Saturday, *in compagnia di alcuni amici*, a cep weighing in at one and a half kilos (over three pounds). It was, concluded the article, a splendid year for fungi and there was good reason to believe that Sra Ceppi's find would prove to be far from unusual. I sat back in anticipation. The polenta appeared: a steaming, corny porridge over whose entire surface tumbled a riot of garlicky, parslied ceps. Halfway through the meal, Dino himself emerged through the swing doors bearing high a basket of *funghi*: magnificent ceps ranging in size from golf balls to boxing gloves. He did a lap of honour of the dining room to accompanying applause, then vanished once more into the kitchen. After everyone had gone, I sneaked into the kitchen after him to see if he would be prepared to divulge the recipe. He was. And he did.

GAME TERRINE

SERVES 8–10

300g/10oz boneless game
150g/5oz chicken livers
150g/5oz boneless fat pork
150g/5oz lean boneless veal or
chicken breast
150g/5oz pork fat
salt and pepper
4 juniper berries
1 tbsp Kirsch
optional: 2 tbsp pistachios
1 bay leaf

An all-purpose game terrine (hare, venison or wild boar could be used) with an optional marbling of pistachios. Plan ahead, as the terrine is immeasurably better if allowed to mature for a few days. Pickled quetsch plums (page 121) make a fine accompaniment.

Trim the game; set aside 6 or 7 strips for the garnish and cut the rest into cubes.

Trim the livers, pork and veal or chicken breast and chop roughly. Chop the pork fat. Put all the chopped meats and fat in a large bowl and sprinkle with salt and pepper. Add crushed juniper berries and Kirsch. Leave to marinate in a cool place for 24 hours.

Finely chop all the meats, except the strips for garnish, using a sharp knife or in a food processor. Stir in the pistachios if using.

Pack half the mixture into a 26 cm/10 inch long rectangular terrine or loaf pan. Lay the reserved game strips on top, then finish with the rest of the meat mixture. Put the bay leaf on top and cover with foil and/or a lid.

Heat the oven to 150°C/300°F/ Gas Mark 2. Put sheets of newspaper in a roasting pan and place the terrine on top.

Fill the pan with water to come two-thirds of the way up the side of the terrine. Bake for about 1 hour until firm and springy, and beginning to come away from the sides. A skewer stuck in the middle will feel uncomfortably warm to the touch. Cool at room temperature, then chill.

Sounding the horns.

CROÛTES AUX CHAMPIGNONS

Mushrooms on Toast

SERVES 4

1 onion, chopped
25g/1oz/2 tbsp butter
450g/1lb mushrooms (wild,
    cultivated or a mixture), sliced
salt and pepper
200ml/7fl oz dry white wine
125ml/4fl oz cream
4 slices of good wholewheat bread
    (eg. Burebrot, page 40)
4 tbsp grated Parmesan or Sbrinz
    cheese

This is wonderful for supper especially if the dish features a selection of fresh field or meadow mushrooms, chanterelles, ceps and saffron milk caps, and the toast is made from Real Bread.

Soften the onion in the butter without browning. Add the mushrooms, season lightly, cover and cook over moderate heat until the juices run. Uncover and cook hard till juices evaporate.

Add the wine and reduce by half. Stir in the cream and simmer for a few minutes more.

Toast the bread and put it in an overproof dish. Spoon the mushrooms over and sprinkle with the cheese. Put briefly under a hot grill (broiler) to dapple with brown.

DINO'S POLENTA E FUNGHI

Polenta with Wild Mushrooms

SERVES 2 AS A MAIN
COURSE

300ml/10fl oz water
200ml/7fl oz milk
salt and pepper
125g/4oz/1 cup quick-cooking
  (2-minute) polenta
1 clove garlic, crushed
25g/1oz/2 tbsp butter
250g/8oz mushrooms, wild or
  cultivated, sliced
chopped parsley
optional: 2 tbsp grated Sbrinz or
  Parmesan cheese

Dino's dish features locally garnered ceps, but cultivated mushrooms can be substituted if you have difficulty finding such treasures.

Put the water, milk and 1 tsp salt in a heavy pan and bring to the boil. Add the polenta and bring back to the boil. Cook, stirring constantly, for 2 minutes. It should be the consistency of creamily scrambled eggs. If too thick, add a little more milk.

In a frying pan, soften the garlic in the butter without allowing it to brown. Add the mushrooms, season to taste, cover and cook for a few minutes until the juices are released. Uncover and cook hard to evaporate the juices. Divide the polenta between two heated plates, top with the mushrooms and sprinkle with parsley and/or cheese. Serve at once.

Rich pickings of saffron
milk caps (*Lactarius
deliciosus*).

ÉMINCÉ DE CHEVREUIL AUX CHAMPIGNONS

Diced Venison with Creamy Mushroom Sauce

SERVES 4

600g/1¼lb boneless tender venison
2 tbsp oil
salt and pepper
2 pinches of paprika
4 juniper berries
50g/2oz/4 tbsp butter
1 shallot, chopped
100g/3½oz mushrooms, sliced
100g/3½oz fresh chanterelles (or use all cultivated mushrooms)
2 tbsp Cognac
200ml/7fl oz beef or game stock
200ml/7fl oz cream
chopped parsley

Any sort of tender game (hare, young wild boar, pheasant etc.) could be substituted for venison, and the mushrooms can be cultivated or wild – or both. Serve with either noodles or rice.

Cut the meat into small pieces and marinate in the oil, salt, pepper, paprika and crushed juniper berries in a cool place for a few hours or overnight.

Heat half the butter and sear the meat on all sides, in small batches, for a few minutes. Remove the meat as it is ready and keep it warm.

In the same pan, melt the remaining butter and soften the shallot. Add the mushrooms, season lightly, cover and cook gently until the juices run. Raise the heat and cook till the juices evaporate.

Add the Cognac, stock and cream, check seasoning and simmer for 5 minutes. Return the meat to the pan and heat through very gently. Sprinkle with parsley before serving.

ROTKRAUT

Braised Red Cabbage

SERVES 8

1 medium red cabbage, about 800g/1¾lb
1 onion, chopped
1–2 tbsp lard or oil
3 tbsp vinegar
1 apple, chopped
salt and pepper
1 tbsp sugar
1 wineglass of red wine
½ wineglass of water
4–5 bacon slices

This dish goes marvellously with game of any sort. The recipe is quite large, but leftovers can be made into soup or frozen.

Quarter the cabbage, remove hard core and shred finely. Soften the onion in the fat, add the cabbage and stir well until glistening.

Add the vinegar, apple, seasoning, sugar, wine and water. Lay the bacon on top and bring to a simmer. Cook gently for about 1 hour or until the cabbage is tender.

FRAU BIRCHER'S HIRSCHPFEFFER

Venison Stew

SERVES 4

1kg/2¼lb boneless stewing game
1 leek, sliced
a piece of celeriac (celery root)
2 carrots, sliced
1 bay leaf
2–3 cloves
2–3 black peppercorns
1 bottle of red wine
1–2 tbsp oil
1 tbsp flour
optional but good: several slices
   dried ceps

Halfway up the mind-bending road from Chur to Tschiertschen is the tiny restaurant Tobelmatte owned by Frau Bircher. She is famous for her typical Graubunden dishes (not least her pear bread, which Prince Charles once ski-ed over from nearby Klosters to sample). Though she makes her stew with red deer meat, other game such as roe deer, wild boar or hare could be substituted.

Trim the game and cut into manageable pieces. Put in a non-metal container with the vegetables, bay leaf, spices and wine. The meat should be completely covered. Leave to marinate in a cool place for 5–10 days. Stir up from time to time.

Lift out the meat and pat dry on paper towels. Strain the marinade and discard the vegetables. Fry the meat, in several batches, in the hot oil in a heavy casserole until lightly coloured. Sprinkle a little flour on the last batch of meat and add the ceps (if using). Return all the meat to the casserole.

Pour on the strained marinade and enough stock to barely cover the meat. Cover and simmer gently for about 1½ hours or until tender.

CHAMPION CHOCOLATE CONSUMPTION

Chocolate is a complicated business. Most people seem to be consumed by guilt at the very thought of it. They furtively buy the odd bar or box, consume the entire contents in one fell swoop and then suffer agonies of remorse. The Swiss, by contrast, seem to be remarkably (one might even say unexpectedly) relaxed about chocolate. They munch their way with apparent insouciance through a staggering ten and a half kilos (around twenty-three pounds) per person per year – a world record. Far from regarding it as sinful, they consider chocolate to be nourishing, even essential, a food, not a fad. A schoolchild's favourite snack before supposedly healthier treats came on the scene was a warm bread roll fresh from the baker, into which a chubby finger would be poked, swiftly followed by a Suchard Branche. After school treats come army rations: the seventeen weeks of enforced military service are presumably made slightly more tolerable by ample supplies of (vitamin-boosted) chocolate from all the chief manufacturers, wrapped in appropriately patriotic paper (red, with a white cross). By the time adulthood is reached, chocolate is a firmly established fixture of Swiss life.

The Swiss had their first taste of drinking chocolate in 1697 when the Zürich businessman Heinrich Escher brought the novel idea

Truffles – the connoisseur's delight.

Autumn chocolates at Teuscher, Zurich.

back from Brussels. It took at least another century, however, before chocolate began to be manufactured locally. Goethe, while visiting in 1797, was apparently so dubious about the quality and availability of Swiss supplies of the beverage that he took with him his own stocks and a private pot in which to brew it up. Initially, chocolate was used for medicinal purposes, available by prescription only and at enormous cost. It was described by a certain Doctor Blancardi in 1705 as 'not only pleasant to taste, but . . . a veritable balm of the mouth, for the maintaining of all glands and humours in a good state of health.' Gradually the idea of eating chocolate for pleasure (rather than drinking it for health) crept across the continent from Spain. By the end of the eighteenth century the Swiss were beginning to take a serious interest in chocolate manufacture, a field dominated at the time by the

Italians. An early *Gastarbeiter* (in reverse), François-Louis Cailler, took himself off to Milan to discover the state of the art. In 1819, back in Corsier on lake Geneva, he opened the first Swiss chocolate factory and set about beating the Italians at their own game. Cailler was a man who understood the intrinsic value of good packaging, and he wrapped his chocolate bars in elegant, gold-embossed paper; on the back, the join was fixed impressively with sealing wax and stamped with his own distinctive seal.

Then came Philippe Suchard, qualified confectioner, tireless traveller, dabbler in asphalt mines and owner of a fleet of boats on lake Neuchâtel. In the 1850s he opened a factory on the shores of the lake. Neuchâtel had belonged to the King of Prussia since 1707 and some of Suchard's best customers (as fond of boating as they were of chocolate) were from the imperial Prussian court, to whom he was soon *chocolatier* by appointment. Later came Charles-Amédée Kohler, whose principal claim to fame was the invention of hazelnut chocolate. Until now, most manufacturers had been situated in the French-speaking part of Switzerland. In 1845 the first factory in the German-speaking part was established by Rodolphe Sprüngli. He saw chocolate as a nourishing food for working people, greatly to be preferred to that all-too-commonly found daily calorie booster of the period: sugared water with *Schnapps*. At the turn of the century a certain Jean Tobler, native of Appenzell, founded the *Fabrique de Chocolat de Berne*; in 1909 the unique Toblerone bar burst upon an unsuspecting world.

The three real chocolate heroes, however, are Daniel Peter, Henri Nestlé and Rodolphe Lindt. Peter distinguished himself not only by marrying into the Cailler chocolate dynasty, but also by discovering how to incorporate milk into chocolate. Nestlé, in turn, made this development possible by inventing the condensed milk which went into Peter's chocolate. Finally – and most importantly – Lindt was responsible for a refinement in the chocolate process known as conching, which removed both the bitterness and grittiness which had characterized the product thus far. His also was the idea of incorporating extra cocoa butter into chocolate in order to give it an even smoother, more melting quality: *chocolat fondant*. Later he sold his process to Sprüngli in Zürich for the huge sum of one and one half million gold francs. The famous partnership of Lindt & Sprüngli was born.

Over the years the familiar old names like Cailler, Kohler, Peter (and latterly Rowntree) have been gobbled up by the huge conglomerate Nestlé, while Tobler has long since belonged to Jacobs Suchard and the whole group was recently ingested by Philip Morris. Lindt & Sprüngli, meanwhile, have held themselves aloof and independent, growing steadily and pursuing quietly their chosen paths of quality and innovation. They recently patented two important new processes in chocolate manufacture. One, known as the Lindt & Sprüngli Moisture Barrier, sounds a bit like a revolutionary new deodorant, but in fact is much more exciting: bite into a Lindt liqueur-filled chocolate and all will become clear. A fragile sugar shell splinters beneath your teeth to release a rush of Kirsch or Williamine which – but for the moisture barrier – would otherwise seep into the surrounding chocolate. Another new process removes the sour and bitter agents from the beans (rather than from the finished chocolate as was previously the practice).

Switzerland imports most of the raw materials needed to make chocolate, from the beans at the beginning of the process to the finishing touches provided by almonds, pistachios, hazelnuts, pine nuts and honey. Only the milk powder and sugar must by law be bought locally in significant quantities (to keep the Swiss farming lobby happy). There are two sorts of cacao beans: Criollo (mainly from Venezuela and Ecuador) are the

aristocrats, and Forastero (mainly from West Africa) are the proles. The key to fine chocolate lies – as with whisky and champagne – in the blending. Both sorts of beans are used, in widely varying (and scrupulously secret) proportions – as I discovered on a visit to the Lindt plant in Kilchberg.

First I watched as the fermented and dried beans were cleaned, roasted and crushed, the husks removed and the resulting powder carefully blended with other similarly treated beans. 'This step,' stressed my charming guide Frau Boenheim, 'is what distinguishes one chocolate from another.' Like a lamb to the slaughter, I innocently enquired as to what proportion of the precious Criollo beans Lindt chocolate might typically contain. There was an embarrassed silence. I felt rather as though I'd enquired of the Princess of Wales where she bought her underwear. (Later I discovered that Lindt's plain chocolate is made exclusively from Criollo beans – no wonder it's so good.)

We moved on to the grinding, when the heat from the rollers causes the mass to melt into a thick liquid mixture and to look and smell (for the first time) reassuringly like chocolate. On cooling it solidifies into cocoa paste, and here there is a parting of the ways. Some of the cocoa paste is pressed to extract the cocoa butter. The resulting (fat-free) cocoa cakes are earmarked for cocoa powder or chocolate drinks. The remaining cocoa paste is the starting-off point for chocolate. In the case of dark chocolate, cocoa butter and sugar are added; in that of milk chocolate, milk powder and a higher proportion of sugar. Technically speaking, white chocolate is not really 'chocolate' at all, since it contains no cocoa paste, only cocoa butter, milk powder and heaps and heaps of sugar. All have to be kneaded (to develop flavour), rolled (to get rid of grittiness) and conched, the crucial stirring stage perfected by Rodolphe Lindt during which the bitterness in chocolate gradually disappears and the flavour develops fully. Finally the chocolate is tempered, a process so delicate that (I was assured) it can quite easily be derailed when the infamous *Föhn* (a disturbing warm wind) blows. (The *Föhn* is blamed for many things in Switzerland.)

Nearing the end of our guided tour, during which I had been bombarded with Lindor balls, plied with liqueur-filled chocolates and tempted by the tiniest Lindt thins, we passed a small room marked *Gewichtskontrolle* (weight control). I wondered nervously if I might be asked to step inside and account for my consumption in the past couple of hours. Seeing my anxious look, Frau Boenheim hastened to explain that it's the chocolates that they like to keep a strict eye on.

Quality control is everything here, as is hygiene: although few chocolates in the Lindt factory are ever touched by human hand (barring occasional manual application of a few decorative violin squiggles of liquid chocolate, or the careful positioning of the odd hazelnut), nonetheless bacterial checks on sweaty palms are made throughout the day. The results are sent up to the laboratory for analysis. If any undesirable bugs are found, the worker will be fined five francs; germ-free palms earn a bonus of ten. It pays to keep clean.

Liquid gold at the Lindt factory.

Some of the most exciting and original chocolates in Switzerland come from the famous *chocolatiers* and confectioners whose tempting displays stud the streets of all Swiss towns and cities. Though few nowadays manufacture their own chocolate from scratch, they are masters in the art of converting top-quality *couverture* (specially tempered confectioners' chocolate with a high cocoa butter content which causes it to melt most obediently) into designer goodies of outstanding quality. Because the product typically contains plenty of fresh cream and butter, it is destined for instant consumption – a stipulation not generally considered to be much of a hardship. Many such businesses were founded in the last century, some are still family-owned and run, each is known for a particular speciality. Sprüngli on Paradeplatz in Zurich, for

The famous Teuscher window dressing.

instance, are renowned for their tiny meringue mouthfuls sandwiched with buttercream (*Luxemburgerli*), while Beschlé in Basle do a brisk trade (including by post for homesick Baslers) in luscious assorted chocolates (*pralinés*) and truffles, as well as their recently patented tangerine-flavoured milk chocolates. The Genevois go to Auer or Arn in the Vielle Ville for their chocolate rations, and of course a stay in St. Moritz would be incomplete without a visit to Hanselmann. The best chocolatiers always have a tea-room attached to the shop. Here you can settle down and thoughtfully work your way through the house selection – a dangerous business, for one

truffle seems somehow to lead always to another . . .

For a total sensory experience, go to Teuscher on Storchengasse in the old part of Zurich. The shop itself is like an Aladdin's cave. The ceiling is hung with huge multi-coloured paper flowers and decorations. Depending on the season (the decor is changed five times a year), shelves and carousels will be covered with witches on broomsticks, sporty figures on skis, frog kings, Santa Clauses or oriental gentlemen. Arms, legs and accoutrements are made of coloured crepe paper, while bodies serve as the housing for selected chocolates, or the famous Teuscher *truffes*.

The latter come in twelve different flavours. I share with the Queen Mother a weakness for the champagne ones: inside an unbelievably fragile chocolate shell lurks a rich, dark champagne-laden truffle filling which in turn encases a nugget of white chocolate. (You don't have to live in Zurich to get Teuscher chocolates: there are shops on Madison Avenue, in the Rockefeller Centre, in Toronto, Houston, Beverly Hills, Tokyo and Singapore.)

At Christmas, consumption rockets. Anything up to a quarter of the chocolate-maker's annual turnover will be concentrated into these few short weeks. Throughout the year, though, they are kept afloat by a steady sale of gift chocolates and personal treats: confectioners (and florists) all over the country must regularly thank their lucky stars that no Swiss would ever arrive for dinner at the home of friends unless armed with a gift (known in Swiss German as a *Mitbringsel*, a 'something-to-take-with-you') of chocolates or flowers. In addition to the usual range, the chocolate-maker will also produce specialities particular to the time of year (Santa Clauses, Easter bunnies), or to the place (bears from Bern, lacy motifs from St Gallen, trout or ducks from Lucerne, watches from La-Chaux-de-Fonds, pine cones from the Jura, steamboats from Schaffhausen). Sometimes there will be exquisite chocolate figures to commemorate events in the city or canton, such as the *marmites* (three-legged chocolate stewpots) filled with marzipan vegetables for L'Escalade in Geneva and the baby *Bööggs* evoking Old Man Winter in Zurich during April.

One of the happiest places to adjourn to for

Inside the Café Schober.

a restorative hot chocolate after some strenuous shopping in Zurich is the Café Schober on Napfgasse. Opened in 1838, it was run until fairly recently by the two Schober sisters, Alice and Ruth. A bell tinkles tinnily as you go in. The scene which greets you is like something straight out of Dickens: chocolates, cookies, cakes, jams, preserves and gugelhopfs are arranged over every available horizontal surface, and dispensed by efficient ladies in lace bonnets and aprons. Your purchases made, you press through to the back where clutches of straight-backed chairs are arranged around minute tables. The walls are decorated with antique chocolate moulds and baking

The chocolate shop at the Café
Schober.

artifacts. There's a buzz of chatter from students from the nearby university, mothers and children out for an afternoon treat, elegantly furred and hatted ladies, well-heeled businessmen and well-advised tourists. The hot chocolate is made from Theodor Schober's legendary home-made product whisked into full cream milk direct from the Schober home farm. If you order an Alice Schober special, it will be further enriched with whipped cream and Kirsch or brandy.

When it comes to 'cooking chocolate', the Swiss are indeed blessed for their own *chocolat ménage* is better than most people's eating chocolate. (Beware of products in other less-favoured countries labelled 'chocolate covering' or 'cooking chocolate'. In these the main ingredients will be cocoa powder, sugar and vegetable fat, with a negligible part played by cocoa butter.) From a visit to Switzerland (and from the following recipes) it will be clear that the Swiss certainly like to cook with chocolate, though they do draw the line at chocolate fondue which they consider an aberration. It's the moist chocolate cakes, airy desserts, crisp biscuits (cookies) and delectable truffles made by Swiss cooks – professional and amateur – which give the real taste of Swiss chocolate.

FRAU BOENHEIM'S CHOCOLATE MOUSSE

SERVES 6

100g/3¹/₂oz Lindt Excellence (or other good-quality dark chocolate)
100g/3¹/₂oz Lindor (or other good-quality milk chocolate)
a small piece of butter
2 eggs, separated
2 tbsp sugar
a pinch of salt
150–200ml/5–7fl oz whipping or double (heavy) cream
grated chocolate
coffee beans

Frau Boenheim looks after visitors to the Lindt & Sprüngli plant. This is her recipe for a gorgeously rich but apparently light chocolate mousse, made from a combination of dark and milk chocolate. Serve it in small, after-dinner coffee cups (demitasses).

Break up the chocolate and melt in a bain-marie or double-boiler. Cool. Stir in the butter. Beat the egg yolks with 1 tbsp sugar until pale and mousse-like. Beat the egg whites with the rest of the sugar until stiff but still creamy. Whip the cream to soft peaks. Fold the yolks into the cooled melted chocolate, then the cream and finally the whites.

Spoon into coupes or coffee cups and chill well. Decorate with grated chocolate and coffee beans.

WHITE CHOCOLATE MOUSSE IN DARK CHOCOLATE BOXES

MAKES 14 BOXES

*1 box Lindt dark chocolate thins
(about 60) or other very thin
dark chocolate squares
200g/7oz white chocolate
a small piece of butter
2 eggs, separated
2 tbsp sugar
a pinch of salt
200ml/7fl oz cream*

Raspberry coulis
*200g/7oz/1¹/₂ cups raspberries
100g/3¹/₂oz/¹/₂ cup sugar*

Another Lindt-inspired dessert, a white chocolate mousse is encased in Lindt thins and served over a fruit coulis. It's quite a fiddly business, but the boxes look stunningly elegant and taste wicked.

Tear off strips of foil and fold them over to make bands the same width as the chocolate squares. Put a sheet of non-stick baking parchment on a small tray or board which will fit in the refrigerator.

Make 14 four-sided boxes with the chocolate squares, bracing them with the foil bands. Fix with staples at one corner.

Melt the white chocolate over very gentle heat in a bain-marie or double boiler. Stir in the butter. Beat together the eggs yolks and 1 tbsp sugar until fluffy. Beat the egg whites with the salt till firm; add the remaining sugar and continue beating till stiff but not granular. Whip the cream to soft peaks. Fold together all four preparations. Spoon the mousse into the boxes. Put them in the refrigerator on their tray/board to set.

To make the raspberry coulis, liquidize the fruit with the sugar and press through a nylon sieve. Spoon on to plates. Lift the mousse boxes with a fish slice (pancake turner) on to the plates, remove foil collars and serve.

Boxes and boxes of
chocolates – ready for despatch.

SCHOGGI-IGEL

Chocolate Hedgehog

SERVES 10–12

250g/8oz dark (semisweet)
chocolate
250ml/8fl oz milk
250g/8oz/2 sticks butter
100g/3¹/₂oz/¹/₂ cup sugar
3 eggs
250g/8oz sponge fingers
(ladyfingers)
100g/3¹/₂oz/1 cup slivered almonds

This Basle recipe is a favourite at confirmation lunches or at Christmas, and consists of a chocolate-flavoured butter-cream layered with sponge fingers (ladyfingers) moulded in an oval dish. To serve, it is turned out and stuck with slivered almond prickles.

Melt the chocolate in the milk. Beat together all but 15g/¹/₂oz/1 tbsp of the butter and the sugar until pale, fluffy and without granules. Beat in the eggs one by one, then the chocolate milk. Leave to cool. Layer the sponge fingers (ladyfingers) and chocolate buttercream in an oval baking dish. Reserve a little buttercream to decorate. Chill.

Toss the almonds in the reserved butter in a heavy pan until lightly toasted. Turn out the dessert on to a serving plate and spread with the reserved buttercream, mounding it up to give a nice hedgehog-like shape. Stick in the almond 'prickles'.

CHOCOLATE TRUFFLES

MAKES ABOUT 40
TRUFFLES

*250g/8oz best-quality dark
(semisweet), milk or white
chocolate*
125ml/4fl oz cream
*Flavourings: 2 tsp honey, or orange
juice, Grand Marnier,
Cointreau, Amaretto, Cognac,
Kirsch or rum.*
*Coverings: cocoa powder, or icing
(confectioners') sugar, hundreds-
and-thousands (candy sprinkles),
chocolate vermicelles, chopped
nuts, crushed praline, melted
chocolate etc.*

A foundation recipe for soft chocolate truffles, on which you can ring the changes almost endlessly: dark, milk or white chocolate, Kirsch or other spirit and different finishing touches.

Break up the chocolate and put in a pan with the cream. Melt over gentle heat, stirring until smooth. Cool the mixture. Stir in the chosen flavouring and beat well with a wire whisk or electric mixer until the mixture lightens somewhat and forms peaks. Chill.

Put the chosen covering in a shallow dish. Form the chilled truffle mixture into balls with a teaspoon or melon baller dipped into hot water. Roll them in cocoa powder (or alternatives) and chill once more. Arrange in a beautiful box and bestow them as a Mitbringsel (gift) on some deserving host or hostess.

CHARLOTTE'S SCHOGGI-TARTE

Chocolate and Hazelnut Cake

MAKES 12–24 SLICES

*150g/5oz dark (semisweet)
chocolate*
2 tbsp water
125g/4oz/9 tbsp butter
6 eggs, separated
*180g/6oz/2 cups ground hazelnuts
or almonds*
1 tbsp Kirsch
a pinch of salt
75g/2½oz/6 tbsp sugar

This outstanding chocolate cake is extremely simple to make and wonderful to eat. For best results, make it at least two days before it is needed and cut in tiny slices as it is very rich.

Heat the oven to 180°C/350°F/Gas Mark 4. Cut a disc of non-stick baking parchment to fit in the bottom of a 26 cm/10 inch springform cake pan. Butter and flour the sides.

Break up the chocolate and put in a heavy-based pan with the water. Melt over very gentle heat, stirring until smooth. Remove from the heat and whisk in the butter and egg yolks. Stir in the hazelnuts or almonds and the Kirsch.

In a large bowl, beat the egg whites with the salt until stiff but still creamy. Add the sugar and continue beating until like meringue. Fold into the chocolate mixture. Tip into the prepared cake pan and bake for about 40 minutes or until risen and firm.

SCHIITERBIIGI

Chocolate Log Dessert

SERVES 4

150g/5oz dark (semisweet)
chocolate
2 tsp instant coffee granules
1 tbsp boiling water
50g/2oz/¼ cup sugar
50g/2oz/4 tbsp unsalted butter
2 eggs
100g/3½oz Petit Beurre biscuits
(or other plain cookies)

The name of this simple and delicious dessert (typically made at girl or boy scout camps) means 'log-pile' – in the construction of which the Swiss are the undisputed world experts. The finished article resembles the best-ordered log pile, with its layers of Petit Beurre biscuits (cookies) sandwiching a rich chocolate, butter, sugar and egg mixture. Another name for it is *Kalti Pracht* – 'faded finery' (the biscuits are usually stale).

Melt the chocolate in bain-marie or double boiler. Dissolve the coffee in the boiling water and add it to the chocolate. Whisk in the sugar, butter and eggs and beat well until thoroughly mixed.

Line a 16 cm/6½ inch loaf pan or terrine with clingfilm (plastic wrap). Pour in a layer of the chocolate mixture, follow with a layer of biscuits (cookies) and so on until all is used up. Refrigerate for at least 2 hours or overnight. Serve with yogurt, or over a fruit coulis or crème anglaise.

FRUITS OF THE EARTH

It is quite possible that William Tell never actually existed, and that all those antics with the apple were simply a figment of Schiller's romantic imagination. No matter. That Switzerland is still automatically associated in people's minds with apples is reasonable enough, since fruit has always played an important part in the diet of this fundamentally farming people. The fruit chapter in a nineteenth-century Swiss cookbook opens with the stipulation that 'on no account should this important food, raw or cooked, be lacking at any meal, for its acid properties are essential to the digestive system.' Today, one of the most lasting and beautiful images of rural, lowland Switzerland is that of rolling green meadows geometrically and systematically planted with cherry, apple, plum and apricot trees, alight in spring with lacy pink and white blossom, and heavy with fruit in the summer and autumn.

The season opens with the cherries, which came to Europe – according to popular legend – courtesy of the gourmet general Lucullus. While battling on the banks of the Black Sea near the town of Cerasus he discovered the sweet cherry tree and marched it triumphantly back to Rome. It was then crossed with the native European wild cherry. The result was the sort of fat, juicy black specimens which are

Apples from Hans Jörg Lauber's
orchard deep in Graubünden.

111

now to be found in all those heroic jams which are an essential part of any pre-skiing breakfast today. In sixteenth-century Switzerland it seems that cherries were deemed to be 'fruit for all' and by law all citizens, rich or poor, could pick wherever they wished. Anyone laying claim to a particular tree was required to mark it with a branch of thorns; subsequent picking from a tree would be treated as stealing and punished accordingly.

Nowadays, though the cherry trees out in the country may look unclaimed (and are seldom fenced off), they are certainly the property of some farming family who would be outraged in the (admittedly unlikely) event of a passer-by helping himself. Cherry-growing is often a small part of the mixed arable farmer's activities. Typically, he will own perhaps a hundred trees of several different varieties (to stagger ripening) dotted about the slopes surrounding the village. Much of the crop will be sold directly from his doorstep: parked outside many an old farmhouse in the villages around Basle from mid-June to mid-July will be an old wooden barrow loaded with weighed and ready-priced cartons of gleaming black and red fruit. Nearby will be a battered tin with a slit cut in the lid, through which customers are trusted to feed their coins.

Work starts early in the year with pruning and carefully controlled spraying – many Swiss fruit farmers subscribe to the principle of 'integrated production', a sort of halfway-house between organic farming and traditional methods of culture. At flowering time – April or May depending on how long winter has lingered – everyone holds their breath for fear of late frosts. The cherry tree (indeed all fruit trees) wisely produces far more flowers than are needed to give fruit – a fact which is not difficult to believe when you look up through its branches at the sheer profusion of brilliant white blossoms set against a pale blue spring sky.

Flowering over, the ripening fruit has to contend with two more potential hazards: cherry-fancying birds with insatiable appetites, and excessive rain which increases the water content of the cherries to such an extent that they burst apart at the seams. The picking is done by (increasingly purple-fingered) family members, often helped by teams of Poles and other east Europeans who return year by year for two weeks' cherry-picking 'holiday'. Girt with a venerable old leather strap to which is attached a picturesque, rounded wicker basket, young and old shin up ladders and painstakingly pick the fruit. As it gets harder to find people who will risk life and limb for a basketful of cherries, attempts are being made to mechanize the harvesting. Low-growing strains are also being bred which can be trained along wires – a development welcomed by the pickers and growers, but regretted by conservationists who fear not only for the graceful, tall old trees, but also for the olive green, red-hatted woodpeckers and other birds who flit happily in and out of their leafy branches.

About twenty sorts of cherry are grown around Basle, with resonant names like Basler Adler, Hedelfinger and Späte Holinger. Undisputed king of them all is the Schauenburger, a variety brought back from the Lebanon at the turn of the century by one Emil Flury, owner of the Hotel Bad Schauenburg near Liestal. A fat, late-ripening cherry distinguished by its brilliant reddish-brown colour and unrivalled flavour, it is probably the one which has done most to establish the reputation of north-western Switzerland as the cherry-growing area of the country (though the people of Zug, whose own excellent cherries make wonderful Kirsch and a memorable cherry cake, might not necessarily agree).

Though many cherry-growers consider that this wonderful fruit is almost too good to cook, Switzerland suffers no shortage of recipes for cherry cakes, tarts, pancakes, fritters and strudels. Often the cherries require stoning (pitting), for which task there exists a nifty device about the size of a hand-cranked mincer (grinder) which is fixed to the kitchen table. The hapless cherries are funnelled inexorably down a slippery slope into a sort of trap. By means of a short karate chop to the lever the stone is blasted out one way, the fruit the other. The economical Swiss even find a use for the stones – after cleaning and drying, they are used as a weight for the blind baking of pastry cases. At a friend's house once in the Valais, I discovered a rough little hessian bag marked *Chirsisteine*, full of rattling cherry stones. Before the advent of central heating (or even hot water bottles), the bag would be placed last thing at night in the residual heat of the wood-burning stove, and later into the bed to warm it up.

Cherries for preserves and distilling require different qualities from table cherries: a thin skin, plenty of juice, intense flavour and a

Cherry trees in the Basle countryside.

slightly bitter finish. One which unites such qualities is the Basler Langstieler, a deep red cherry which has been established in the area for at least three hundred years and whose wonderful aroma withstands even the rigours of the preserving pan or the village still. Few farming families actually make their own Kirsch nowadays; the *Brennrecht* (right to distil), formerly passed down by inheritance and obscurely linked to the number of cows on the farm, is being gradually phased out. Nowadays most people take their bins of fully fermented cherries to the local expert, to re-emerge in the form of a powerful, clear white spirit, beautifully bottled and decoratively labelled with the grower's name.

The production of Kirsch is of course not left entirely in the hands of cow-owning farmers and smaller producers; it is also the domain of some well-known professionals. One of the best-known names is Dettling, a family concern which has been producing fine Kirsch at Brunnen in canton Schwyz in the heart of Switzerland since 1867. A bottle of Dettling Kirsch contains nothing but the best hand-harvested Swiss black cherries — between twelve and fourteen pounds are needed to make one bottle. The cherries are fermented and the mash left in sealed containers to rest and mature. When the time is ripe, it is moved over into the firm's beautiful old copper stills reserved exclusively for the making of Kirsch (to avoid any exchange of flavours with other fruits) where it is distilled gently and slowly at very low temperatures, thus enabling all the fragrance of the fruit to be preserved. Only the heart of the matter (known as the middle run) is kept; the first and last runnings (also known as foreshots and feints) are discarded. Dettling's standard Kirsch is aged for three to four years in 50-litre demijohns in special ageing rooms; their aptly named *Réserve Exceptionelle* is aged at least ten years.

Consumption of Kirsch, unlike that of other spirits, is relatively stable, probably because only about a third of it is consumed straight. The rest is used as what is described, presumably tongue in cheek, as an *Aromaverstärker* (flavour enhancer), and splashed liberally into desserts, chocolates, cakes, jams, *Fasnachtskiechli* and fondue.

The famous Dettling Kirsch.

Sandwiched briefly between the cherry crop and the apple and pear harvest come all the stone fruits (fruit with stones/pits). Along the sun-baked Rhône valley floor in late July the roads are lined with stalls selling crates of pinkish-gold Luizet apricots for provisioning the picnic basket, or for jam, pies, sorbets, ice creams and (in our household) chutneys. Around the corner where the Rhône widens into lake Geneva, the gently sloping orchards lend themselves more to peach and plum culture.

The plum family is a little less demanding than its hot-house cousins and thrives from lake Geneva up the whole length of the Jura chain to Basle, and around to lake Constance. Mirabelles, greengages and quetsches are the more familiar sorts; rarer are the old varieties like Bérudge, Damassine (not, as you might expect, a damson but a small, sweet plum unique to a little enclave in the northwest of Switzerland called the Ajoie, where it is made into a powerful *eau de vie*); and Marchissy, from the village above lake Geneva of the same name. Of all the plums, the quetsch, descended from the prickly sloe (*Prunus spinosa*) and the cherry plum (*P. cerasifera*), is by far the most important, and perhaps the 'most typically Swiss'. They can be eaten raw, but are most often cooked in a variety of dishes. André Maurois called them 'mussel plums', which describes them beautifully: inside their blackish-blue housing the flesh is yellow and sweet.

First on to the market in mid-August are the little blue Bühlers, followed by the fat Fellenbergs (also known as *italienische Zwetschge* because their original homeland was Lombardy). Though the bulk of the crop ends up in the distillery as *Zwetschgenwasser* or *eau de vie de quetsche*, there still seem to be plenty left over for an impressive range of tarts, cakes, compotes, mousses, ice creams, jams, pickles and preserves. Quetsches are sometimes dried on the prune principle, subsequently to enliven a winter stew or soup; when cooked to a paste with Kirsch, sugar and cinnamon, layered with an almond butter filling and wrapped in pastry, they form part of the classic *Glarner Pastete*, a speciality of the pastry-cooks of canton Glarus.

Open-faced quetsch tarts are a fixture of the early autumn calendar, made alike by housewives and professional bakers and often served for supper with a big cup of milky coffee. The plums are halved, stoned and snipped down the middle (so they don't turn inside out in the heat of the oven) and covered in a creamy custard. Home-made ones will usually be rectangular, occupying an entire oven baking sheet – the ones supplied with Swiss ovens have raised edges for this purpose. Bakers' tarts (traditionally a Friday special: 'if it's Friday it must be pie day!') are usually round and baked in quiche pans.

In the old days, a piece of leftover yeast dough would be used for pastry, which greedily sucked up the plum juices; nowadays it's much more likely to be a delicate short-crust or an elegant puff pastry. Most celebrated of all are the *gâteau aux pruneaux* served throughout the French-speaking part of Switzerland on the day of the *jeûne fédéral* (the Federal Fast) in mid-September.

'Apples', claims fruit- (and wine-) grower Hans Jörg Lauber, 'are the people's fruit ('*Volksfrucht*') – you can take them anywhere, eat them on a ski lift, or tuck them in your rucksack before setting off for a mountain hike. Pears, however, are a *Kulturfrucht*: you need patience to grow them, knowledge of when to pick them, a knife to peel and quarter them, and a good piece of cheese to go with them!' At the foot of his beautiful old onion-domed house in Malans (Graubunden), he grows fifteen different sorts of apple and three sorts of pear – 'about ten too many', he grins ruefully, reflecting that the average consumer doesn't know even a quarter of them.

Apple trees adorn almost the entire Swiss lowland landscape, but the biggest concentrations are found in the Valais, around lake Geneva in canton Vaud and lake Constance in canton Thurgau. First on to the market in the late August are early sorts like the nicely acidic Vista Bella and the reddish-gold Gravensteiner (a formidable distilling apple giving an *eau-de-vie* of the same name). They are briefly interesting and designed for quick consumption. Then come the autumn sorts (Cox's, Kidd's Orange, Spartan, Berner Rosen) whose complexion remains unwrinkled until about Christmas time. Last of all come the storage sorts which can safely be kept in the fallout shelter (mandatory in all Swiss homes of recent construction) for several months. These include the best-selling Jonathan, the firm cooker Boskoop (of the russet type), the aptly named Glocken or 'cowbell apple', and superbly fragrant, sweet-sour Maigold. In the spring, when the supermarkets are wheeling

Precarious apple-picking in Graubünden.

out the last tired crates, Maigold is the only one to have conserved something of its autumn aroma.

Golden Delicious dominates the market in Switzerland as comprehensively as anywhere else and makes up about a third of the total crop. Its only redeeming feature seems to be its numerous and distinguished Swiss offspring (Arlet, Maigold, Elstar and Jonagold, to name but a few), all of which have thoroughly upstaged their rather dull parent. Switzerland, as befits a country with an apple consumption second to none, is constantly developing new varieties, notably at the research institutes in Wädenswil and Changins. My vote goes to the spirited Rubinette, described as a *Zufallsämling* (a chance seedling), which defied the white-coated scientists and spontaneously did its own thing very successfully (admittedly with a bit of help from a Golden Delicious and a Cox's Orange Pippin).

Pears, as you might expect of such a cultured fruit, are more discreetly represented on the market than apples and also grow extensively in the Rhône valley and up around lake Constance. Fruit growers seem to concur that while Conference sells well, there's nothing to beat the brown-skinned Kaiser Alexander or the pale yellow Comice. William's (Bartlett) pears are almost all distilled, while good old Louise puts in fairly frequent appearances. *Eierbirnli* ('egg pears') are an old variety seldom found but worth seeking: about the size of a small egg, they are cooked or preserved and served with game.

Defenders of the old, fast-fading fruit varieties will rejoice to know of the existence of a Swiss organizationn called Fructus. Similar to the Brogdale Horticultural Trust in England, their aim is to keep these old sorts alive by formulating an inventory, setting up a gene bank, and sponsoring exhibitions and fruit shows.

At one held recently in Liestal near Basle the air was perfumed with Blenheims, Bismarcks, Bienenbergers and Boskoops. Down one wall a veritable A to Z of apples from Arlet to Zapfenapfel was ranged in nesting boxes like new-laid eggs; down another were almost as many pear varieties. Alongside curiosities like the little Lederapfel – inedible raw because of its leathery skin, but wonderful cooked and served as the typical accompaniment to *Metzgete* – was the nicely-named Schafnase (sheep's nose) and the grandmotherly Grossmutterapfel. The prize for the prettiest went to the Usterapfel, a tiny golden ornament worthy of a Christmas tree. People thoughtfully tasted slices of apple and pear proffered by fresh-faced young fruit farmers, then bought big bags of assorted fruit to try out at home. The coffee corner did a brisk trade in apple cakes and pear tarts, juice and *Schnapps*.

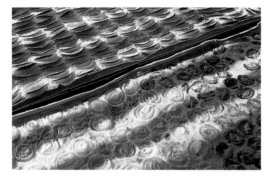

Apple and pear recipes are legion. A simple but original Swiss supper dish (often served as a main course with milk coffee, followed by bread and cheese) is apple '*Rösti*', also known as *Apfelbröisi* or *Oepfelchrauschi*. Slices of apple are tossed in a pan with lightly fried cubes of stale bread, sugar and sultanas (golden raisins) or raisins. Apple sauce is an essential antidote to the richness of sausages, or the slight astringency of liver patties; it is served even with polenta. From Geneva comes the recipe *poires à rissoles* in which pears are cooked to a thick paste and then incorporated into little pastry turnovers. In neighbouring Vaud, a curious product called *raisiné* is to be found. It consists of a stern reduction of apples and pears which looks a bit like molasses and is used for desserts in combination with cream, eggs and sugar.

A few nice old fruit-related traditions persist. In those villages which still have a press, a typical Saturday afternoon pastime is to fill up the car boot (trunk) with pails of surplus fruit from tired old fruit trees (ideally a mixture of apples and pears, of which special juice sorts exist) and take them down to be made into juice. Another old tradition was the drying of fruit and vegetables to last for the winter, a task originally carried out in the attics of the grand old farmhouses, later in the village drier (of which some are still in use), and nowadays at home in a multi-layered machine which looks a bit like a steamer. The flavour is deliciously intensified and the resulting wrinkled slices are used for schooltime snacks or cooked into a *potée valaisanne*, incorporated into a fruit bread or added to a braised piece of bacon to give the dramatic-sounding dish *Schnitz und Drunder*. Maybe somewhere in Switzerland some schoolchild still observes the time-honoured practice of depositing a burnished apple with the baker on the way to school, to retrieve it later baked inside a golden cloak of crisp pastry.

In spite of earnest attempts on the part of the *régie fédérale des alcohols* to keep fruit out of the still, nonetheless a certain quantity of apples and pears escapes the net and ends up as wonderful clear fruit spirits, much enjoyed for medicinal purposes, or added to coffee (for a mountain-top *Kaffee fertig*) or poured over ice cream. Apple spirits range from the ominous-sounding *Träsch*, or *öbschtler* to the more specific *Gravensteiner*. In the Emmental, a good meal would be incomplete without a shot of *Bätzi* to follow. Pears end up as the incomparable Williamine for which the Valais is justly famous.

Switzerland's
best on display
in the old
quarter of
Lugano.

SCHNITZ UND DRUNDER

Pears and Apples with Potatoes and Bacon

SERVES 4–6

1 onion, chopped
25g/1oz/2 tbsp butter
1 pear, peeled, cored and sliced
1 apple, peeled, cored and sliced
optional: 1 tbsp sugar
salt and pepper
500g/1lb 2oz potatoes, peeled and
  roughly chopped
a 300g/10oz piece of bacon or ham
2 tbsp cream

The combination of apples and/or pears with potatoes and smoked pork in a savoury one-pot meal crops up all over German-speaking Switzerland under many different names. In the old days, the fruit would have been dried, the potatoes from stocks in the cellar and the bacon or ham from the family pig.

Soften the onion in the butter without allowing it to brown. Add the pear and apple and toss them in the sugar (if using). Season lightly and add potatoes and enough water to barely cover. Cut the bacon or ham into large chunks and add to the pan.

Simmer for about 30 minutes or until most of the liquid has evaporated. Stir in the cream, check the seasoning and serve immediately.

119

CANARD RÔTI AUX CERISES DE SCHAUENBURG

Roast Duck with Cherry Sauce

FOR 4 PEOPLE

salt and pepper
2 Sauvagine ducks
1 onion, finely diced
1 carrot, finely diced
4 shallots, chopped
75g/2¹/₂oz/6 tbsp butter
20 cherries
2 tbsp Cognac
250ml/8fl oz dry white wine
3–4 tbsp cream

A recipe from chef Patrick Labalette of the Gasthof Bad Schauenburg, *alma mater* of the Schauenburg cherry. The ducks are pinkly roasted, carved and served over a sensational cherry-red sauce. Use pigeons (squabs) – one per person – if Sauvagine ducks (a cross between wild duck and Barbary) are unavailable.

Heat the oven to 200°C/400°F/Gas Mark 6. Season the ducks. Put the diced vegetables in a roasting pan and put the ducks on top. Roast for 15–20 minutes: they should remain pink inside. Carve the thigh and breast meat and keep it warm.

Put the chopped carcasses and vegetables in a saucepan, barely cover with water and simmer for 15–20 minutes. Strain, return to the pan and reduce to about a cupful. Reserve this stock.

Soften the shallots in 25g/1oz/2 tbsp butter, then add the stoned (pitted) cherries, Cognac, wine and duck stock. Season to taste and simmer gently for 10–15 minutes. Put in the blender and liquidize till smooth. Return to the pan, check seasoning and whisk in the cream and remaining butter, cut into pieces. Divide sauce between four heated plates and arrange carved duck on top. Serve with wild rice and a purée of small white turnips.

Succulent plums on display at Basle's open air market.

VALLY STERN'S KIRSCHPFANNKUCHEN

Cherry Cake

SERVES 6

3 stale milk bread rolls (about 175g/6oz)
about 250ml/8fl oz warm milk
3 eggs, separated
100g/3½oz/½ cup sugar
100g/3½oz/1¼ cups ground almonds
grated zest of 1 lemon
ground cinnamon to taste
a pinch of salt
about 800g/1¾lb cherries

A quick and easy cherry and almond cake, this is delicious served warm or cold, either as a teatime cake or for dessert with a little vanilla ice cream.

Butter a 26 cm/10 inch round cake pan. Heat the oven to 170°C/325°F/Gas Mark 3. Break up the rolls and soak in the milk until soft. Mix or process till smooth with the egg yolks, sugar, almonds, lemon zest and cinnamon. Beat the egg whites with the salt until stiff but still creamy. Fold them into the almond mixture along with the cherries (no need to stone/pit them). Pour into the prepared pan and bake for about 1 hour or until firm.

ESSIGZWETSCHGEN

Pickled Plums

MAKES 4 × 450g/1lb JARS

1kg/2¼lb quetsches or other plums
500g/1lb 2oz/2½ cups sugar
200ml/7fl oz vinegar
200ml/7fl oz red wine
3 cloves
a little ground cinnamon
2 tsp salt

Pickled quetsch plums go wonderfully with game dishes, meat pies, cold meats or *pot-au-feu*. The recipe is adapted from *die Herstellung von Konserven* published in 1905.

Prick the plums several times with a needle. Put the sugar, vinegar, wine, cloves, cinnamon and salt in a wide shallow pan and bring to the boil. Lay in the plums and simmer gently for a few minutes till they lose a little colour and begin to split. Remove the pan from the heat and leave the plums to infuse till next day. Lift them out with a slotted spoon and put them into jam (canning) jars. Boil up the juice until somewhat reduced and well-flavoured. Pour it over the plums and close the jars tightly. Keep several months before broaching.

FRAU WIRZ'S BLACK CHERRY JAM

MAKES 5–6 × 450g/1lb JARS

*2kg/4¹/₂lb black cherries, stoned
(pitted)
1kg/2¹/₄lb/4¹/₂ cups sugar
juice of 2 lemons
optional: 3–4 tbsp Kirsch*

Frau Wirz and her family own a large fruit farm above Reigoldswil in the picturesque Basle countryside. She likes to spike the finished jam with a little of their own Reigoldswiler Kirsch. If using preserving sugar (which has inbuilt pectin – a good idea with cherries to ensure a good set), follow the instructions on the packet.

Put the cherries in a preserving pan with the sugar and lemon juice. Allow to stand for about 2 hours or until the juices run. Bring to the boil over fierce heat. Cook at a galloping boil for 16–18 minutes, or until setting point is reached: put a saucer in the freezer for a few minutes, remove and pour in a little jam. Pull your finger through it: a distinct channel should form. If not, boil for a few minutes more. Remove from heat and stir in Kirsch if using. Pour into jam (canning) jars while still hot and cover at once with lids or cellophane discs.

Black Cherry jam, home-patted butter and freshly baked bread for the best Swiss breakfast.

122

MAMA RUTH'S 'APPLE STRUDEL'

SERVES 6–8

1kg/2¼lb assorted apples (Cox's,
  Maigold, Russets)
2 tbsp sugar
grated zest and juice of 1 lemon
3 tbsp ground almonds or hazelnuts
3 tbsp raisins or sultanas (golden
  raisins)
250g/8oz puff pastry
breadcrumbs
butter

In Graubunden, the Austrian influence is ever-present in cooking. In this version from Ruth Lauber in Malans, selected apples are grated, mixed with raisins and spices and rolled up in (bought) puff pastry – less demanding than the traditional strudel paste and just as good. Optional extras are vanilla or cinnamon ice cream, or *crème anglaise*.

Heat the oven to 200°C/400°F/Gas Mark 6, preferably with bottom heat only. Grate the unpeeled apples coarsely and mix with the sugar, zest, juice, nuts and raisins. Roll out the pastry to a large rectangle. Put it on a floured tea-towel. Sprinkle with breadcrumbs and dots of butter.

Arrange the apple mixture over half the surface of the pastry (the long edge). Roll up like a Swiss (jelly) roll, curve around into a horseshoe shape and put on a baking sheet. Bake in the lower part of the oven for 30–40 minutes or until golden brown and crispy.

GÂTEAU AUX PRUNEAUX

Quetsch Plum Tart

SERVES 4–6

250g/8oz puff or shortcrust (basic pie) pastry
3 tbsp ground almonds
about 900g/2lb quetsches, halved and stoned (pitted)
5 tbsp sugar
Optional:
1 tsp vanilla essence (extract)
3 eggs
200ml/7fl oz cream

Ground nuts on the bottom of fruit tarts help protect the pastry from the juice. The recipe is for quetsch plums, but could be adapted to use almost any fruit: stoned (pitted) cherries or apricots, or peeled and sliced apples or pears – all would be delicious. The custard finish is optional.

Roll out the pastry to fit a 28 cm/11 inch quiche pan. Heat the oven to 200°C/400°F/Gas Mark 6, if possible using bottom heat only. Scatter ground almonds over pastry and lay in the fruit, cut sides up, using it to brace the pastry sides. Sprinkle on 2 tbsp sugar and bake for 20 minutes. If using custard, mix together the vanilla, eggs, cream and remaining sugar and pour on to the fruit. Bake for a further 15–20 minutes or until set. Alternatively, bake the tart for about 35 minutes without the custard.

THURGAUER APPLE SPONGE CAKE

SERVES 4–6

125g/4oz/10 tbsp sugar
125g/4oz/9 tbsp butter
grated zest and juice of ¹/₂ lemon
3 eggs, separated
125g/4oz/1 cup flour
a pinch of salt
1 tsp baking powder
3 small tasty apples (e.g. Cox's,
   Russets etc.)
2 tbsp slivered almonds
icing (confectioners') sugar

Halved, thinly sliced apples nestle in a lightly lemony sponge cake with spikes of almond and a dusting of sugar on top. For best results, be sure to use a well-flavoured, non-collapsible apple.

Butter and flour the sides of a 18 cm/7 inch springform cake pan. Cut a disc of non-stick baking parchment to fit the bottom. Heat oven to 180°C/350°F/Gas Mark 4.

Beat together the sugar and butter until thoroughly creamy and light. Add zest, juice and egg yolks. Sift together flour, salt and baking powder. Beat the egg whites until stiff but still creamy. Fold the flour and whites alternately into the butter mixture. Peel, halve and core the apples, then slice almost through. Spoon the batter into the pan. Push the apple halves into batter, five around the edge, one in the centre. Scatter the almonds on top.

Bake for 30–40 minutes until golden and firm and a skewer stuck in the middle comes out clean. Cool, then sprinkle with icing (confectioners') sugar.

Freshly picked apples for an apple sponge.

A TASTE OF SWITZERLAND'S WINES

Wandering one warm summer's evening through the vineyard village of Chexbres above lake Geneva, we spotted a notice in a wine grower's window. On closer inspection, it turned out to be a message from Montaigne written on his travels around Europe in the seventeenth century: *Il faut apprendre à connaître les vins du pays où l'on se trouve. C'est la meilleure manière de pénétrer dans l'intimité profonde d'une terre ...''* A more elegant and poetic way to invite travellers to taste the local fruits of the vine would be hard to imagine. We accepted the invitation, and have been digging deeply into the intimate depths of Switzerland's wines ever since.

Switzerland is a wine-growing and a wine-drinking country. In the French- and Italian-speaking cantons, as well as further north in the German-speaking areas, there are interesting and worthwhile growers to be found, and wine finds to be made. Many Swiss wines never make it beyond the confines of the canton, let alone the country – which makes Montaigne's advice all the more apposite. For openers, try a crisp, thirst-quenching Chasselas or a nicely aromatic Riesling-Sylvaner. Then treat yourself to something special, like an Arvine from the Valais or a Pinot Gris from Graubunden. Instead of drinking Bordeaux in Biasca or Beaujolais in Bern, why not see what Switzerland can do with Merlot, Pinot Noir and Gamay on her own ground?

Terraced vineyards in the Valais.

successfully ageing some of their Pinots in new oak. Not to be disdained is Dôle blanche, a delicate, lightly pressed rosé in which Pinot Noir predominates and whose colour varies from deep honey to the palest onion skin tint.

Monsieur Zufferey is a specialist of two ancient red Valais grapes which produce wines of real body and longevity, perfect partners for the rich game dishes for which this hunting canton is famous. Cornalin (Rouge du Pays/Landroter) is an extremely rare variety produced in tiny quantities. It is an awkward grape to grow, performing in effect only once every three years to give a wine of deep colour, bags of body, masses of nicely spiced fruit (especially cherries) and sufficient tannins to guarantee it a good long life. Red Humagne (no relation of the white) is thought to be Oriou from the Val d'Aosta just over the other side of the Matterhorn. Tough and tannic in its youth, it rewards keeping by developing considerable finesse with age. Newly introduced red varieties in the Valais which are worth looking out for include Syrah and Nebbiolo.

At the top of the valley in Visp is Josef-Marie Chanton, a young grower who has worked tirelessly to rescue from oblivion a series of near-obsolete varieties of the upper Valais. We sampled them in the cavernous depths of his cobwebby cellar on the Junkergasse. Some, he cheerfully admits, are more worthwhile than others. Gwäss (Gouais blanc) and Himbertscha were both common a hundred years ago in the Valais when sharp, thirst-quenching wines were required for the arduous work in the vineyard. Gwäss has little aroma, and seems sharply reminiscent of cider.

Himbertscha is more flowery but still with high acidity. Its name sounds temptingly reminiscent of raspberries, but is apparently derived from a word in the upper Valais dialect meaning 'on the trellis', a reference to the way the vines were trained in former times. Next came Lafnetscha (the Blanchier from neighbouring Haute Savoie), whose name is also derived from the dialect. It could loosely be rendered as 'don't drink me too early' — which is good advice, for the wine is very tough when young and is tamed only with age, developing a faint suspicion of elderberries.

Heida (Païen) is the star of these old varieties, a distant cousin of Savagnin (of *vin jaune* fame). We later drove up the winding road to Visperterminen to see the vertiginous vineyards where it is grown at almost a thousand metres. The Chanton Heida is a wine of real class: deep straw-coloured, it is powerfully aromatic with good acidity. (Heida is often subtitled *Gletscherwein*, but should not be confused with the *vin de glacier* from the adjacent Val d'Anniviers, an oxidised curiosity made in a solera system and offered by the thimbleful to honoured guests and visiting firemen.) With some stunning Gewürztraminers and Malvoisies (Pinot Gris) we were back on familiar (read Alsace) ground again but with a subtle, Swiss difference. A wonderful Pinot Noir, deep cherry red, toasty and chewy, and a robustly tannic red Humagne completed the tasting. Supper chez Chanton, just below the beautiful medieval church which Rilke wisely chose as his last resting place, was a memorable feast of wild asparagus and Arvine, both from Josef-Marie's vineyards.

VAUD

For sheer breathtaking beauty and precision planting, the *vaudois* vineyards are hard to beat. Banked steeply up from lake Geneva and graced by the occasional elegant eighteenth-century summer house, they gaze proudly out across the water to the Dents du Midi and distant Mont Blanc. 'Nothing,' commented the famous French viticulturalist Jules Guyot in 1860, 'is better planted, laid out, propped up, lined up, pruned, pared, tilled, weeded and manured than a Swiss vine beside lake Geneva.'

This is Chasselas country *par excellence*. Some growers dabble with other white varieties (Pinot Gris, Pinot Blanc, Riesling, Chardonnay, Sylvaner, even Gewürztraminer) but you sense that their heart is not in it. 'Why change?' asks Marco Grognuz of La-Tour-de-Peilz, near Villeneuve. Why indeed. With their image of quality and finesse, *vaudois* Chasselas fetch a good price on the domestic market, and on the strength of little more than word-of-mouth recommendation and a terse, photocopied list, most growers systematically sell out their entire production within about six months of bottling. Red wine production is on the up; Pinot Noir and Gamay fight it out here, sometimes compromising in a (usually unimpressive) blend known as Salvagnin, sometimes coming (more impressively) into their own as varietals. A few privileged souls even benefit from a spell in a new oak.

The Vaud vineyard, which hugs the lake in a huge arc around from near Montreux to just

Vineyards near Chexbres overlooking lake Geneva.

The Gut Plandaditsch in Malans, Graubünden, home of the Lauber family.

GERMAN-SPEAKING SWITZERLAND

If you followed the Rhine all the way from its emergence in Graubunden up through St. Gallen and into Lake Constance, out again through Schaffhausen, Aargau and finally to Basle you would (with a side-step down to lake Zurich) have taken in most of the principal vineyards of German-speaking Switzerland – and enjoyed a very scenic route into the bargain. This is the land of treasured, manicured vines netted and guarded by bird-frightening machines, their leafy skirts lifted at summer's end to maximize sunshine to the ripening grapes. Later they will be harvested by family and friends, the products available only within a small radius of the vineyard.

In this part of the world Müller-Thurgau (known in Switzerland simply – and rather

disloyally, since Herr Müller was a Swiss from Thurgau – as Riesling-Sylvaner) takes over from Chasselas as the main white wine grape; Pinot Noir (Blauburgunder) is officially the only red variety. The whites can, in the right hands, be deliciously aromatic and surprisingly good; the reds (often known as *Landwy* – country wines or *Beerliwein*, 'berry wines') tend to be pale and slightly fizzy: *nicht jedermann's Sache* (not everyone's idea of fun), though much enjoyed as local quaffing wines.

Hans Jörg Lauber, wine (and fruit) grower at the beautiful, onion-domed Gut Plandaditsch in Malans (Graubunden) provides good evidence of what can be done in the superb microclimate of Malans, one of the 'gentlemens' villages' (known collectively as the *Bündner Herrschaft*) famous for their rich, well-structured wines. Here the warm *Föhn* wind, far from being feared for its customary headache- and suicide-inducing qualities, is valued as an aid to early ripening and is referred to as *der Traubenkocher*: the grape cooker. Hans Jörg's Pinot Noirs are meaty, his Pinot Blancs strongly aromatic, his Pinot Gris rich and smoky, his Chardonnays (eked out by the six-bottle case to selected customers) firm and memorable. Thanks to him I had my first taste of Freisamer, a delicious cross between Sylvaner and Pinot Gris which his pioneering father introduced to the area.

Around the corner is the Gasthof Ochsen owned by the Donatsch family. Here you can settle down on the terrace overlooking the rooftops of the elegant patrician houses, wrap yourself around a bowl of pearl barley soup studded with chunks of *Bündnerfleisch* and wash it down with a glass or two from the Donatsch family's small but significant production. Their Pinot Gris comes close to the best from Alsace; their oak-aged Pinots are terrific, toasted to a turn by the *Föhn* and discreetly woody. Herr Donatsch speaks respectfully of the old variety Completer (its name supposedly linked to the evening service of compline, after which the grateful monks would quaff a glass or two). It is a rare and ancient variety found only in Graubunden and around lake Zurich, whose tardy ripening makes it a tough proposition for these northerly climes.

While in these parts, take time to look in at the Hotel Stern in Chur, hidden away in the picturesque back streets of this ancient episco-

The Schlossgut Bachtobel, canton Thurgau, surrounded by Hans-Ulrich Kesselring's vineyards.

pal town. The hotelier, Emil Pfister, is as enthusiastic and well-informed a guide as you could wish to find to the wines and food of Graubunden, both of which are served with considerable expertise in the cosy, pine-panelled dining room of his lovely old inn.

Further north, canton Thurgau which skirts lake Constance is the home not only of Herr Müller of that ilk, but also of Hans-Ulrich Kesselring. At weekends he dons his black wine grower's apron and conducts samplings of Schlossgut Bachtobel's wines for the private customers who make up the bulk of his clientèle. We joined the local doctor and a publisher of art books on the garden wall one warm, misty autumn morning. At our feet lay the gently undulating Thurgauer landscape, and in the distance snow-capped Säntis loomed. Bachtobel Riesling-Sylvaners are austere, as might be expected this far north, and given the clay soils on which they are grown; the reds (about eighty per cent of the Schloss's production) are a world apart from the usual northerly Swiss Pinots: chewy, with real substance and not a trace of fizz. They can be found on the wine list of the storybook village inn next door, the Weinberg, or at the Schäfli in nearby Wigoltingen.

Over in Würenlingen in neighbouring canton Aargau, Anton Meier runs one of the foremost vine nurseries in Switzerland, owns the village inn (the Sternen) and makes some outstanding wines of his own. His Riesling-Sylvaner is aromatic and lively, putting paid to the received view that this grape can never be anything but a dreary workhorse. His Pinot

Noir (recently placed at the head of a list of Pinots from all over the world in a blind tasting organized by the prestigious wine magazine *Vinum*) is one of Switzerland's most convincing. Try it with his long-marinated, richly braised beef (*Suure Mocke*) for a rare treat.

On the edge of lake Zürich, only the road along the 'Gold Coast' (the northeastern side of the lake) separates Hermann Schwarzenbach's beautiful old half-timbered house from the water. Opposite lives the fisherman, behind the house the vines are banked steeply upwards. Tasting is conducted not from a vat but actually inside one: it's turned on its side, you clamber in and sit at a little candle-lit table. Schwarzenbach's Riesling-Sylvaner is another good example of what this grape can give, his Räuschling (an old lake Zürich variety) is crisp and steely, tailor-made to go

with the fisherman's catch. Here Pinot Noir is known as Clevner (or Klevner), a little thin in poor years but worthwhile if the weather is kind.

Heading back towards the Basle area, a small diversion off the motorway brings you to the village of Ueken near Frick. Here is to be found the double act of Fehr and Engeli. Bruno Fehr used to make his living at one of the big chemical firms in Basle while his partner Emil Engeli kept the home fires burning. Their wines (Riesling-Sylvaner, Blauburgunder from various sites and a rosé) are now so successful that Bruno has taken early retirement and devotes himself exclusively to the business – look out for their wines in the wine bar of the Teufelhof in Basle, or chez Stucki on the Bruderholz (for whom they make a special *cuvée* of non-malolactic Riesling-Sylvaner, a rarity for Switzerland, where almost all wines systematically undergo secondary fermentation). Finally, just outside the small village of Aesch near Basle are to be found the vineyards of Vordere Klus, owned by Kurt Nussbaumer. Arranged around a sun-baked natural 'amphitheatre', the vineyards are helpfully signposted to indicate which grape varieties are planted, with pointers on how to recognize them by their foliage. Down below in a hollow, surrounded by vines, nestles the family restaurant where in addition to the usual Riesling-Sylvaner and Blauburgunder, you can sample Herr Nussbaumer's excellent Pinot Gris and Gewürztraminer. Of more recent date is his *méthode champenoise* Chasselas known as *Chrachmost* which has ousted champagne as the house aperitif.

The wine matures.

136

TICINO

The picturesque pergola culture once favoured by growers in the Italian-speaking part of Switzerland is fast disappearing – as are the traditional grapes like Bondola, Freisa and others which once adorned them. In their place has come Merlot, which now comprehensively dominates the Ticinese wine picture. A straight Merlot del Ticino is usually smooth, mild, not especially memorable. Exciting wines are being made by top people like the venerable Valsangiacomo family in Chiasso and Vinattieri Ticinesi in Ligornetto. Also notable are a handful of young growers fresh from the viticultural schools of Changins or Wädenswil, refugees frequently from the frozen (German-speaking) north, their minds untrammelled by traditional ways of doing things, their benchmark the best Bordeaux. Many, such as Werner Stucky in Olivone and Erich Klausener in Purasca, are using new oak barrels to give their Merlots the dimension they previously lacked.

After a tour of Vinattieri's impressive new winery – sparkling stainless steel vats under giant roofs suspended on huge wooden beams, whole hillsides newly transformed from scrubby woods into gently sloping, pebble-strewn vineyards – lunch at a *grotto* was mooted. We wound our way up the Monte Generoso through sun-flecked chestnut groves, past the cep seekers and the red-stock-inged walkers. Marcello Brissoni, the sales manager, talked energetically and persuasively of oak, Oechslé levels, tannins and Château

Ticino tipico.

137

Petrus. One hand was occasionally attached to the steering wheel of his BMW, the other was mostly engaged in dialling the *grotto* on the car 'phone to warn of our impending arrival and to ascertain what was on the menu today. '*Stinco di maiale con polenta!*' came the uncompromising response. It turned out to be a slowly stewed shin of pork in a rich sauce with chunks of polenta, over whose angular edges gorgonzola gently slithered. We sniffed and sipped at Vinattieri's house wine, even at this relatively humble level no stranger to oak.

Before leaving Ticino, a visit to the legendary Angelo Conti Rossini in Brissago is a must. Tiring of the grand, elaborate and expensive dishes he used to prepare in his own restaurant (and latterly as chef at Giardino, page 147), he decided to open a small place called Osteria Agora, where, inspired by the Greek example, people would come together to put the world

to rights over a plate of food and a glass of wine. The atmosphere is appropriately agoraesque: seated at a long refectory table next to the polyglot fisherwoman's son in his knitted hat may be found visitors of various nationalities or native wine-growers, discussing subjects as diverse as the latest catch of *pesce persico* (perch), the rising Deutschmark, or the timing of this year's harvest. Angelo's food is intensely flavoured, rustic, served with quiet flair: a slice of tuna terrine maybe, or palest green ravioli with a splash of tomato sauce, followed by spoon-tender braised beef and polenta flecked with little black buckwheat specks, and *torta di pane* (see recipe page 45). The wines are carefully chosen as representative of the true Ticino – a drop of Giovanni Caversazio's sunbaked Merlot Tre Terre from Verscio is memorable even after you have scurried back to the frozen north.

Trellised vineyards above Locarno, lake Maggiore.

AARGAUER SUURE MOCKE

Wine-braised Beef

SERVES 4–6

1kg/2¼lb boned piece of braising
  beef, rolled and tied
1 bottle of robust red wine
3 tbsp wine vinegar
1 onion, sliced
1 carrot, sliced
a piece of celery stick, chopped
1 clove garlic
1 clove
1 bay leaf
1 tsp black peppercorns
a sprig of sage
1 tbsp oil
1 tsp tomato paste
1 tsp flour
salt and pepper
12 prunes, stoned (pitted)

This typical dish of beef braised in red wine is served at the Gasthof Sternen in Würenlingen with the *patron's* Pinot Noir. The prunes give a sweetish contrast to the sharp sauce; provide a further foil in the form of a creamy purée of potatoes and celery root (celeriac) or white turnip.

Put the beef in a non-metallic container with the wine, vinegar, onion, carrot, celery, garlic, clove, bay leaf, peppercorns and sage. The meat should be completely covered with liquid. Leave for at least a week in a cool place, turning occasionally to ensure even marination.

Remove meat, pat dry with paper towels and season. In a heavy casserole, sear the meat in hot oil on all sides. Boil up the marinade and strain. Stir the tomato paste and flour into the casserole and cook for a few minutes, then add the strained marinade. Bring to a simmer, season to taste, cover and cook gently for 1½ hours. Add the prunes and continue cooking till tender. Remove strings from the beef, slice thickly and return it to the casserole. Serve with the prunes and cooking juices.

THE ART OF
THE SWISS HOTELIER

'Deliver us from storms, robbers, plagues, drunken soldiers, false soothsayers, devils in hermits' disguise, and, if need be, from murderous innkeepers, and avalanche, flood and earthquake!' So reads the slightly breathless inscription on the wall of an ancient Swiss roadside chapel. Although avalanches and floods still tragically occur, earthquakes nowadays are mercifully rare, and innkeepers seldom murderous. For today's traveller, drawn to Switzerland by the promise of its calm continental climate, commendable law and order, squeaky-clean atmosphere and utter peace and quiet, it is hard to imagine what can have prompted such a heartfelt

supplication. Yet even a hundred and fifty years ago, the country must have shown a very different face to its visitors.

Until the late eighteenth and early nineteenth centuries, the Swiss countryside was grindingly poor, families were huge, beggars were commonplace. The lowlands were inhabited by farmers, the lakeside villages by fishermen and part-time wine growers. The Alps were considered – with good reason – to be thoroughly menacing. No-one in their right mind would have considered scrambling among them for pleasure, far less taken it into their heads to want to conquer them. Then came the Romantic movement. Rousseau

Switzerland's most famous attraction, the Matterhorn.

philosophized from his adoptive Geneva on man's perfect nature in an imperfect world; Byron waxed lyrical over the Château de Chillon; Goethe chronicled his extensive travels through the country; Turner captured on canvas the astonishing changes in colour, light and weather in the mountains. Switzerland became suddenly *de rigueur*, a mandatory stop on the well-bred nineteenth-century traveller's itinerary. For centuries, hospitality had been dispensed by the hospices on the mountain passes, by convents and monasteries, or by the village priest or local farmer. For the swelling numbers of visitors in search of pleasure, meditation, learning – and comfort – this was no longer enough: the golden age of Swiss hotel-keeping had begun.

Names like César Ritz ('King of hoteliers, and hotelier of kings'), Alexander Seiler (whose family history is in many ways that of Zermatt and of the Matterhorn) and Johannes Badrutt (father of winter tourism, architect of the Cresta run, and importer of curling to Switzerland) became legendary. In 1844, the first edition of the Baedeker guide claimed that 'without a doubt, Switzerland possesses the finest hotels in the world ... It is rare to come across a really bad inn.' Fifty years later C.E. Montague, the English novelist and essayist, concurred that 'the Swiss are inspired hotel-keepers', but put things in perspective by adding that 'some centuries since, when the strangers strayed into one of their valleys, their simple forefathers would kill him and share out the little money he might have about him. Now they know better. They keep him alive and writing cheques.'

Though the aims of today's hotel-keeper – which certainly include keeping his guests alive and well and working hard on their cheque books – may seem at first glance to be fairly standard, Swiss hotels fall nonetheless into a number of satisfyingly diverse categories. The Grand Old Swiss Hotel, for instance, is the place to spend a honeymoon night, conduct a mad idyll or conclude the business deal of the century. Then there is the mountain hotel, whose job it is to pamper weary skiers, walkers and climbers after a strenuous day's exercise. The lake-side hotel provides a haven from the storm, ideal for the jilted lover or the novelist suffering from a temporary bout of writer's block. A certain sort of Swiss hotel is really a restaurant *avec chambres*: here the emphasis is on the stunning food, while the rooms are designed principally to lodge the satisfied diner. Perhaps most genuinely Swiss of all are the small village inns, often family-run, and – at their best – perfect examples of Swiss hospitality.

Some of the staff at these hotels – whether on duty at the reception desk, or responsible for food and beverages, or behind the scenes in the kitchens – may have been lucky enough to train at one of Switzerland's world-famous hotel schools. Here a full-blown hotel management course costs approximately the same as an MBA at a top business school, equips students with an impressive range of skills for all areas of the hotel business and provides an almost cast-iron guarantee of life-long employment in a profession which has always enjoyed singularly high esteem in Switzerland: that of hotelier.

GRAND HOTEL VICTORIA-JUNGFRAU

3800 INTERLAKEN

The Victorian-Jungfrau, epitome of the grand old Swiss hotel.

The Victoria-Jungfrau is the essence of the Grand Old Swiss Hotel. She breasts the Höheweg, Interlaken's Piccadilly, her yellow and white striped awnings suggesting a ship in full sail. Across the tree-lined street, stretching out before her like a private park is the Höhematte ('high meadow') where even today a few Swiss cows still obligingly graze. From the hotel – thanks to the foresight of those who decreed over a century ago that this precious meadow might never be built on – is an astonishing, uninterrupted view of that other famous lady, the Jungfrau.

Originally there were two fairly modest hotels on this site: the Pensionshaus Jungfrau and the Pension Victoria. In 1856 a young, energetic entrepreneur named Eduard Ruchti bought the Victoria and between the autumn of 1864 and July 1865, with the help of architects Friedrich Studer and Horace Eduard Davinet, he completely rebuilt it, elevating it resoundingly from the ranks of mere pension to that of hotel. (In spite of its name, Queen Victoria never actually stayed here, even in its latter, grander days. The story goes that she was not amused that a (then) rather second-rate pension had had the temerity to use her name. Ruchti, however, shrewdly realizing the importance of the almost exclusively English tourist trade at the time, kept the name and took care to find a place for her statue in the park of the hotel.) In 1895 he bought the neighbouring Jungfrau (designed also by Davinet and therefore homogenous in style), crowned the central section in 1899 with a beautiful tower and christened the whole stunning neo-baroque ensemble the Grand Hotel Victoria-Jungfrau.

One hundred and twenty-five years on, it's still stunning. Upstairs the bedrooms (each with its own brass doorbell) are arranged around an elegantly balustraded central well. Downstairs, in the imposing, domed Salon Napoleon the chandeliers sparkle, the silver glints. For elegant dining there is the conservatory-style restaurant La Terrasse; for

143

Swiss specialities there is the cosy Jungfrau-Stube; and for sportsmen (the hotel has several indoor and outdoor tennis courts) there is the Racquet Club with an emphasis on healthy eating. The Victoria-Jungfrau is the only place I know in Switzerland which serves a decent cup of tea (with milk, not cream) – and, on request, paper-thin cucumber sandwiches. In 1875, Ruchti had the revolutionary idea of installing passenger lifts, followed in 1882 with the introduction of electricity. 1992 will see the opening of a complete health and beauty centre in the basement to bring the hotel fully up to the standards expected of five-star guests. The Victoria-Jungfrau may be a grand old lady; but like the best and most worthwhile of old people, she has kept herself interesting, up-to-date – and very, very beautiful.

SEILER HOTELS
3920 ZERMATT, VALAIS

Two things dominate Zermatt: the Matterhorn and the Seiler family. The Matterhorn is certainly the older of the two but without the drive and vision of the Seiler family, hosts to Edward Whymper at the time of his ill-fated first ascent of the mountain, it might never have become so famous. Ironically (and rather gruesomely), nothing served the cause of Zermatt's publicity so well as the dramatic plunge to their death of four of Whymper's fellow climbers; Zermatt was well and truly on the map, success for the Seiler family hotels was assured.

The Monte Rosa, Edward Whymper's favourite watering-hole.

Hotel Riffelalp, Zermatt.

Alexander Seiler's first hostelry was a three-roomed village inn named the Monte Rosa, leased in 1853 from the local doctor. Soon the capacity was extended to thirty-five beds and the hotel became a byword with the budding band of mountaineers who began to flock to Zermatt to climb the 'four thousands' – the twenty-nine peaks over four thousand metres high which surround the village. When asked for a recommendation on where to stay in Zermatt, Whymper would unfailingly reply: 'Go to Seiler's, to the Monte Rosa.' The following year Seiler took over a mountain inn on the Riffelberg high above Zermatt and in 1884 the majestic Hotel Riffelalp was built on this superb site.

Of the six hotels operated nowadays by the Seiler family in the village, the original two still hold a special fascination. Those with a head for history will be attracted to the Monte Rosa, only a short ride from the railway station in the hotel's burgundy-coloured horse-drawn sleigh or carriage (Zermatt is a car-free resort). To step inside the *Salon des Alpinistes* on the first floor (also known as the *Salon Whymper*) is like taking a step back into the last century: the wood-panelled walls are hung with sepia photographs of guests and mountain climbers, famous and not so famous. Lace curtains hang before the windows, occasional tables are scattered with newspapers, a faint smell of pipe smoke lingers; you almost expect to find antimacassars adorning the plumply upholstered chairs. The dining room is long and low, with peach-coloured curtains and twinkling chandeliers. It is the room from which Whymper hurriedly planned his ascent of the Matterhorn after he had learned of his colleague and (former) friend Carrel's treacherous decision to attempt the climb without him, from the Italian side.

Those with a head for heights may opt for the Riffelalp, set on a shelf some two thousand metres up from the village. As you trundle

upwards on the rack railway (or toil upwards on foot) take time to marvel not only at the breathtaking scenery, but also at the sheer audacity and vision – some might say madness – of Alexander Seiler who built his hotel up here in the late 1880s when the only way to reach it was on foot – or by mule if you were fortunate and/or rich. Not only was there no railway up from the village, even the train from Visp to Zermatt was as yet unbuilt. In spite of its inaccessibility, the intrepid English visitors were so numerous that a small Anglican chapel was built to take care of their spiritual needs. It still stands below the hotel, a little the worse for wear nowadays but a reminder of times gone by when the alps were overrun by hordes of mountaineering-mad British.

The grand old Riffelalp burned down in 1961. From its ashes rose, in 1988, the present twenty-room mountain hotel. It is the sort of place which should be stayed in at least once a year by anyone living a mad, bad life permanently suspended between plane seats and car 'phones. Perched on its wide shelf (alight in summer with wild flowers, in winter deep in snow), it is the place to adjourn to with a good pair of walking boots (or ski gear), plenty of suntan cream, a pair of binoculars (for spotting climbers on the Matterhorn), some excellent reading material and several decks of cards for Canasta sessions in the evening. There are no packaged tourists, just a few like-minded people, the occasional bird, miles and miles of walking tracks and ski pistes, a tennis court which claims to be the highest in Switzerland – and everywhere the Matterhorn.

HAUS PARADIES
7551 FTAN, ENGADINE (GRAUBUNDEN)

There are many ways to get to *Paradies*. Some people swing up the winding road from Scuol in sleek motor cars, others call ahead to announce their arrival by train and are met off the little red Rhätische Bahn by a member of staff in the hotel Range Rover. For those who failed to take such precautions, there is always the post bus which is synchronized with Swiss precision to meet the train and take them up the hill. The first time we went there, we arrived on foot, equipped with wicked appetites and having feasted our eyes en route on views of Schloss Tarasp far below in the valley, on carpets of summer wild flowers and on distant mountain peaks. To their undying credit, the staff of the hotel, headed by Brigitte Jöhri, managed to look as though people regularly arrived footsore and travel-stained for lunch in *Paradies*. The staff have an astonishing, collective ability to make you feel as though you're the one guest they've been waiting for all day, all week, all year . . .

The hotel stands on an outcrop some distance from the village of Ftan – the name comes from the latin *vetonium*, meaning sheeps' meadow. Where sheep once grazed, now you're more likely to glimpse the local policeman's goats (which provide both meat and cheese for the *Paradies* kitchen), a few grey-brown cows, the odd roe deer or the occasional walker. The building, though modern, is decorated in a warm, understated way; you feel more as if you have strayed into

a private house than checked into a hotel. On the first floor there's a well-stocked, polyglot, panelled library complete with Bechstein grand and volumes of Chopin, as well as a writing room beautiful enough to tempt even the most reluctant letter-writer to put pen to paper. In summer, instead of pompous florists' bouquets, the house is decorated with bunches of fresh wild flowers and grasses from the surrounding meadows. The bedrooms are comfortable rather than luxurious; the spotlight is uncompromisingly on the food.

It is no coincidence that *Haus Paradies* is sub-titled *Hotel und Restaurant des Gourmets*. House guests are treated nightly not to the standard hotel *demi-pension* fare, but to a *menu dégustation* composed according to what is freshest and best today. Dinner is served in the cool elegance of the all-white dining room, one side of which is entirely taken up

View of the valley from the dining room in the Hotel Haus Paradies.

with huge picture windows giving a privileged view of the mountain peaks to the other side of the Inn valley. In the *à la carte* restaurant (for non-residents), you can choose between various *menus dégustation*, or a lobster tasting menu based entirely on the beast, or – perhaps most interesting of all for visitors to Switzerland – the chef's 'traditional Bündner dishes newly created'.

Graubunden is rich in game and wild mushrooms; on his day off, the chef can sometimes be spotted slipping off with his basket to a secret rendezvous with some ceps, or with his rod and keep-net to catch fresh-run trout in a nearby mountain stream. Autumn tasting menus may feature all three – fish, game and wild mushrooms – woven together into a thoroughly harmonious ensemble. The wine list is full of the inevitable French treasures as well as a selection of wines from small, quality-seeking Swiss growers such as Thomas Donatsch in Malans (see page 134). The Italian pages are unusually good, and the wines from Valtellina (which, as Veltliner, used to belong to Graubunden) worth investigation.

As we reached the end of a long, late, lingering lunch, joyful noises (in Spanish) could be heard upstairs in reception. Through the dining room doors streamed several generations of Latin Americans, from granny in her eighties down to the smallest two year-old. Was there any possibility of lunch (by now it was about 3.45 p.m.)? Brigitte Jöhri beamed delightedly, armfuls of coats were whisked away, menus were brought, a high chair procured and lunch ordered. In *Paradies*, hospitality is clearly a twenty-four hour business.

ALBERGO GIARDINO
6612 ASCONA, TICINO

'Spring is sprung', read the note which accompanied the box of camellias and mimosa delivered by the postman one grey Friday morning in Basle. 'When may we expect you?' If Hans Leu, owner and director of Giardino in Ascona is in the habit of sending such propositions to potential guests at the end of a dreary winter, it is little wonder that the hotel enjoys a ninety per cent occupancy rate during the ten months in which it is open.

It took me till autumn to follow up the invitation. Down through the Gotthard the vineyards were just turning to gold, the Ticino alps were faintly powdered with snow, lake Maggiore lightly ruffled by the rough north winds of the season's tail end. Upon arrival at the long, low-slung, pink-painted *albergo*, a glass of champagne is pressed into the guest's hand to ease the pain of registration. Ushered upstairs to the bedroom, the door closes behind you with a satisfying intake of breath and a pleasing thud. You survey the four-poster bed, the smooth linen sheets, the gently enveloping duvets, the sofa for lounging. Over on the table rests a basket of grapes and fresh figs (the latter an essential antidote to the sybaritic lifestyle which can play havoc with the system, not to mention the figure). The bathroom is a sea of rich red marble, set about with acres of dressing gowns and towels. Next door is that aristocrat of loos, the Closomat. It reaches parts which others definitely never do. Even a telephone is thoughtfully provided,

The pink *palazzo*: Albergo Giardino.

mounted on the wall within arm's reach — for emergencies perhaps (particularly if you failed to read the Closomat instructions properly), or for calling up your friends to tell them all about it.

Out in the garden, tennis courts are intermittently and automatically sprinkled with water, grateful gardens are splashed by fountains, swimming pools are gently warmed, the golf course is within spitting distance (except that no-one here would dream of doing anything so inelegant). A fleet of pale pink bikes stands at the ready before the front door, urging you to a little leisurely cycling. There are daily outings in the pink post bus to picnics by the lake or in the wood with a (downhill) walk promised for the return. In the basement is the *Giardino di Bellezza*, an entire beauty centre offering unlimited opportunites to be pummelled, pampered, massaged and manicured.

Housed in a Roman bath-like room is a Turkish bath, sauna and whirlpool.

Giardino has two restaurants: da Bruno, open throughout the week to house guests and non-residents from Wednesday to Sunday; and Aphrodite, principally for residents, which provides stunning breakfast buffets, light lunches and tempting dinners. At da Bruno, resident chef Bruno Keist prepares elegant, beautifully balanced dishes with a fishy, rather French emphasis. In the Aphrodite dining room it is easy to believe the boast that the staff/guest ratio is one to one: fleets of young people in broad-shouldered Armani-style jackets and amusing ties scurry about attending to the diner's every need. The food falls into three categories: home (Italian) cooking, elegant food, and healthy eating. You can mix and match the dishes to create your own menu. Dishes are discreetly portioned (bearing in mind that the full meal includes six courses — more than enough for anybody), easy on the eye and tempting to the palate.

The indefatigable owner Hans Leu emphasizes in conversation the importance of atmosphere in a hotel. Giardino's is young, fun, unpompous, unmistakeably rich but definitely not glitzy, a sort of Mediterranean-style villa with a healthy dose of Swiss perfection. The attentiveness of the staff helps too, as does champagne at every turn and facilities which combine those of a gym, sports centre, spa, health hydro, concert hall and theatre all rolled into one. When spring is sprung (or when news of that unexpected legacy from great aunt Jocelyn drops on the mat), it's a great place to go.

SEILER HOTELS

RIFFELÄLPER KÄSESCHNITTE

Baked Cheese Toast

SERVES 4

300g/10oz Gruyère cheese
100g/3½oz Appenzeller cheese
2 eggs
6 tbsp dry white wine
grated nutmeg
salt
4 chunky slices of good bread
2 pears, peeled,
halved and cored
gherkins or cornichons
pickled onions

If you take the two-hour walk up to the Riffelalp from Zermatt (rather than the twenty-minute train ride), a restorative baked cheese sandwich from young chef Thomas Moor is indicated on arrival. Served on the terrace with a view of the Matterhorn, it tastes wonderful.

Heat the oven to 200°C/400°F/Gas Mark 6. Grate both cheeses and mix with the well beaten eggs and 2 tbsp of the wine. Season with nutmeg and a little salt. Sprinkle the bread slices with the rest of the wine, place half a pear on each one, and top with the cheese mixture. Bake till golden brown and bubbly. Serve with gherkins or cornichons and pickled onions.

SWISS 'FRENCH' DRESSING

MAKES ABOUT
450ml/15fl oz

1 tsp salt
plenty of ground black pepper
1 tsp mustard
300ml/10fl oz olive oil
100ml/3½fl oz vinegar
1 tsp sugar
1 egg or 2 tbsp cream
stock or water

This makes a creamy, fairly thick dressing which should be kept in a screwtop jar in the refrigerator and used within 3–4 days. If you prefer not to use a raw egg, cream can be substituted.

Blend together all the ingredients except the stock or water in a blender or food processor until quite smooth. Add enough stock or water to give a lightly coating consistency. Put in a screwtop jar and keep in the refrigerator. Use within 3–4 days.

SEILER HOTELS

COUPE MATTERHORN

Not so much a recipe, more an essential experience for ice-cream lovers and a favourite with Riffelalp guests: vanilla, chocolate and chocolate chip ice creams are piled high, bathed in whipped cream, doused in chocolate liqueur and served with hot chocolate sauce.

The chocolate pudding that tops all others.

HAUS PARADIES

GIALUN DA CUNIGL TRAT CUN APRICOSAS SECHAS

Boned Rabbit Legs with Dried Apricots

SERVES 4

4 hind legs of rabbit (about 180g/6oz each)
4–6 dried apricots
salt and pepper
2 tbsp oil
4 tbsp white wine
150ml/5fl oz well-reduced jellied veal stock
25g/1oz/2 tbsp butter, cut into pieces

One of Roland Jöhri's 'recreated' Graubunden dishes: partially boned rabbit legs are larded with strips of dried apricot, pan-roasted and served with a sternly reduced veal and white wine sauce. Serve with steamed vegetables and polenta (page 93, minus the mushrooms) or *Spätzli*.

Remove the thigh bones from the rabbit. Cut the dried apricots into strips. Make incisions in the meat with the point of a sharp knife and insert the apricot strips. Season the rabbit legs and fry them in hot oil, turning once or twice, for 12–15 minutes. Remove from the pan and keep them warm. Tip away any fat from the pan. Deglaze with the white wine and allow to reduce to about 1 tbsp.

Whisk in the stock and reduce to about 4 tbsp. Whisk in the butter bits, then check seasoning. Divide the sauce between four heated plates. Slice each leg into 4 pieces and arrange over the sauce.

151

ALBERGO GIARDINO

AGNOLOTTI CON BARBABIETOLE E RICOTTA MAGRO CON SALSA DI RADICE DI PREZZEMOLO

Pasta parcels with beetroot and quark filling
and a parsnip sauce

This colourful vegetarian dish is a speciality at da Bruno

Make the pasta dough with the flour, egg yolks, oil, a good pinch of salt and enough water to make a dough. Knead well until smooth and not excessively sticky – add sprinkles of flour if needed.

Peel the beetroot and chop finely. Mix with the soft cheese and season to taste with salt and pepper.

Soften the shallot in a little of the butter. Add the parsnip, moisten with the stock and boil hard to reduce by half. Add the cream and simmer gently until slightly thickened. Purée until smooth in a blender. Return to the pan and whisk in the remaining butter. Taste and adjust the seasoning. Keep warm.

Peel the carrot and cut it into tiny dice. Blanch and drain.

Divide the pasta dough in half and roll both out very thinly. Place heaped teaspoons of the beetroot and cheese filling over one half of the dough, leaving space around them. Wet the spaces between the mounds of filling, then place the remaining dough over and press down around the filling to seal. Cut out rounds, with the filling in the centre, using a pastry cutter or glass.

Cook the agnolotti in boiling salted water until just al dente (4–5 minutes). Drain well.

Pour the sauce onto plates and arrange three or four parcels on top. Garnish with the diced carrot and parsley. Serve immediately.

SERVES 4–6

250/8 oz/1²/₃ cups plain (all-purpose) flour
6 egg yolks
1 tsp olive oil
salt and pepper
150g/5oz cooked beetroot (beets)
100g/3¹/₂ oz/¹/₂ cup low fat soft cheese (quark)
1 small shallot, chopped
50g/2oz/4 tbsp butter
200g/7oz parsnip, peeled and diced
150ml/5fl oz vegetable stock
250ml/8fl oz double (heavy) cream
1 carrot to garnish
sprigs of parsley to garnish

POSTSCRIPT

The Swiss are crazy about salads. Almost every meal starts with a freshly-prepared salad, in summer or winter, whether at home or in the office canteen, in a skiers' mountain-top restaurant or the village inn.

The choice of ingredients is wide, the quality outstanding. A green salad may contain (besides lettuce) cress, lamb's lettuce (mâche), oak leaf, cut-and-come-again salad leaves, green chicory or portulaca (purslane); a mixed salad is limited only by the imagination of the chef and by the season, and may include various differently coloured chicories and endives, beetroot (beets), kohlrabi, fennel, celeriac (celery root), tomato, cucumber, sweetcorn, cheese, hard-boiled egg, radishes (red and white) and cabbage (ditto), *sauerkraut*, sweet peppers (red, green and yellow) . . . Usually there will be a choice of three dressings: 'French' (a creamy dressing, for which the recipe is given on page 150), 'Italian' (a straight vinaigrette) and Roquefort.

BIBLIOGRAPHY

Borer, Eva Maria, *Tante Heidi's Swiss Kitchen*, Nicholas Kaye Ltd., London 1965

Bosshard, Anna, *Bürgerliches Kochbuch*, Schulthess & Co, Zürich 1934

Bradfield, B., *A pocket history of Switzerland*, Schweizer Spiegel Verlag, Zürich 1966

Bührer, Peter, *Schweizer Spezialitäten*, Albert Müller Verlag, Rüschlikon-Zürich 1986

Caselli, Giovanni & Sugden, Keith, *Ancient Pathways in the Alps*, George Philip & Son Ltd., London 1988

Coradi-Stahl, Emma, *Gritli in der Küche*, Kommissionsverlag von Rascher & Cie. 1909

Ecole professionelle Richemont, *La Boulangerie Suisse*, Richemont Luzern 1983

Gaulis, L. & Creux, R., *Swiss Hotel Pioneers*, Ed. de Fontainemore (SNTO) 1976

Guggenbühl, Helen, *Schweizer Küchenspezialitäten*, Schweizer Spiegel Verlag, Zürich 1956

Guidicelli, Maryton & Bosia, Luigi, *Ticino a tavola*, Corriere del Ticino, Lugano 1976

Jöhri, Roland, *Die Kochkunst Graubündens*, AT Verlag, Aarau 1989

Kaltenbach, Marianne, *Ächti Schwizer Chuchi*, Hallwag AG, Bern 1977

Kaltenbach, Marianne, *Cooking in Switzerland*, Impressum Verlag AG, 1985

Kelly, Sarah, *Festive Baking in Austria, Germany and Switzerland*, Penguin Handbooks, 1985

Merz, Michael & Brüllman, Dave, *Kulinarische Reise durch die Schweiz*, Schweizer Illustrierte, Ringier AG, Zürich

Meuth, Martina and Neuner-Duttenhofer, Bernd, *Schweiz, Küche, Land und Leute*, Droemer Knaur, Munich 1989

Montandon, Jacques, *Le Jura à table*, Editions Pro Jura, Moutier 1975

Poltéra, Maggie, *Das Kochbuch aus Graubünden*, Verlag Wolfgang Hölker, Münster 1979

Rochaix, Michel, *Vignes et vins de notre pays*, Editions Mondo SA, Lausanne 1977

Saucisses de chez nous, Schweizerischen Fachschule für das Metzgereigewerbe Spiez

Standen Hazelton, Nika, *The Swiss Cookbook*, Atheneum, New York 1977

La Suisse Gourmande, Nestlé S.A., Vevey

Swiss National Tourist Office, *Out of the ordinary Swiss museums*, SNTO Zürich

Switzerland (8th edition), Michelin Tyre PLC, 1985

Tour de Suisse des vins Band 1–5, Fachverlag Schweizer Wirteverband 1983–85

Vignes et vins de notre pays, Ed. Mondo Lausanne, 1977

Wermuth, Sophie, *Die Junge Köchin, Lehrbuch für Koch- und Haushaltungs-Schulen*, Basel 1908

FOOD AND WINE MUSEUMS IN SWITZERLAND

Of the many museums for which Switzerland is renowned, the following
may be of interest to the gastronomically inclined:

F o o d

Alimentarium,
Musée de l'Alimentation,
1, rue du Léman,
1800 Vevey
(Nestlé-funded food museum)

Schweizerisches Freilichtmuseum für ländliche
Bau- und Wohnkultur Ballenberg,
3855 Brienz
(practical demonstrations of cheese- and bread-
making in old, reconstructed houses)

Nationales Milchwirtschaftliches Museum,
3117 Kiesen (near Thun)
(Dairy)

Musée Suchard,
22, rue du Tivoli,
2003 Neuchâtel
(chocolate)

Jacobs Suchard Museum,
Seefeldquai 17,
8034 Zürich
(coffee)

Maison du Blé et du Pain,
Place de l'Hôtel de Ville,
1040 Echallens
(bread and baking)

Swiss Gastronomy Museum,
Schloss Schadau,
3600 Thun
(the library features some of the Harry Schrämli
collection of cookbooks)

W i n e

Musée vaudois de la vigne et du vin,
Château d'Aigle,
1860 Aigle (near Montreux)

Musée de la vigne et du vin,
Château de Boudry
2017 Boudry (on lake Neuchâtel)

Rebbaumuseum am Bielersee
2514 Ligerz (on lake Biel)

ACKNOWLEDGEMENTS

Thanks are due to many people who helped in the preparation of this book, not least to:

Erica Rokweiler who generously lent her polyglot library of cookbooks and patiently ploughed through the manuscript;

to Mme Isabelle Huguenin of the Swiss National Tourist Office in Zurich, Frau Helga von Graevenitz of the Tourist Office in Basle, Herr Hans Stucki of the Restaurant Bruderholz, Signor Angelo Conti Rossini of the Osteria Agora in Brissago and Herr Emil Pfister of the Hotel Stern in Chur for advice, contacts and ideas;

to Herr Georg Corrodi and Frau Boenheim of Lindt & Sprüngli, and to Herr Felix Daetwyler of the Café Schober and Teuscher chocolates for insights into Swiss chocolate;

to Marlis and Hansueli Hofer in Schleumen for an unforgettable bread baking session, and *Ämmitaler Schöfigs* for lunch;

to Susi and Andreas Putzi, incomparable guides to the alpine cheese, air-dried beef, pear bread and wines of Graubunden;

to Frau Egli of Glauser in Basle, for the loan of her cheese library and a guided tour of mountain cheeses;

to Christophe von Ritter of the Société des Exportateurs de Vins Suisses for invaluable advice on Swiss wines and growers;

to Herr Hans-Ruedi Schaub, the itinerant butcher, whose skill with the knife is unerring and whose sense of humour never fails;

to Dr. Peter Gutzwiller, Jagdleiter of the Liestal Jagdgesellschaft for information on hunting and an invitation to the Treibjagd;

to Chosy and Marlis Chanton for vinous weekends in the Valais and a memorable asparagus feast;

to Herr Ernst Schläpfer of the Basle Fruit- and Wine-growers Association and Herr Hansruedi Wirz in Reigoldswil for cherry tips and apple information;

to Messrs Blattner, Knapp and Latscha, the mushroom men, for patiently identifying my funghi finds in German, French and/or Latin;

to Ettingen's butcher, baker and cheese-maker; Herr Stadelmann for patiently assembling sausages and cold cuts; Herr and Frau Thuring and Christoph, for baking a series of special breads for photography and enduring us under their floury feet in the bakeshop; and Herr and Frau Flückiger for allowing us to trip up their customers with tripods and dealing patiently with requests for yet more cheese amongst the Friday morning *Milchhüsli* crush.

The Publishers gratefully acknowledge the support of Arnold Dettling in the making of this book, and would like to thank the Swiss National Tourist Office for their kind permission to reproduce the photographs on pages 14, 18 and 22. Charlotte Wess provided the flower illustrations.

Author's note on recipes

Flour is plain white (all-purpose), sugar is caster (superfine) and cream is whipping unless otherwise specified.

INDEX